UNIQUE

PERSONALIZE YOUR HOME

HOMES

THROUGH GOOD DESIGN

COLLINS DESIGN

An Imprint of HarperCollinsPublishers

UNIQUE HOMES: PERSONALIZE YOUR HOME THROUGH GOOD DESIGN
Copyright © 2006 by COLLINS DESIGN and Carol Soucek King

HarperCollins books may be purchased for educational, business, or sales promotional use. For information, please write: Special Markets Department, HarperCollins Publishers Inc., 10 East 53rd Street, New York, NY 10022.

First Edition

First published in 2006 by:
Collins Design
An Imprint of HarperCollins *Publishers*
10 East 53rd Street
New York, NY 10022
Tel: (212) 207-7000
Fax: (212) 207-7654
collinsdesign@harpercollins.com
www.harpercollins.com

Distributed throughout the world by:
HarperCollins International
10 East 53rd Street
New York, NY 10022
Fax: (212) 207-7654

Art Director and Graphic Design:
Agnieszka Stachowicz (ag_stach@yahoo.com)

Library of Congress Cataloging-in-Publication Data

King, Carol Soucek.
  Unique Homes : Personalize your Home through Good Design/Carol Soucek King.-- 1st ed.
     p. cm.
  ISBN 0-06-082049-7 (hardcover)
  1. Interior decoration--Psychological aspects. I. Title.
  NK2113.K46 2006
  747--dc22
                              2005024016

Produced by Crescent Hill Books, Louisville, KY.
Printed in China by Everbest Printing Co.
First Printing, 2006

DEDICATION

TO THOSE WHO UNDERSTAND THAT OUR HOME IS OUR OWN PERSONAL STAGE – OUR OWN PRIVATE UNIVERSE IN WHICH TO EXPRESS OURSELVES WITH CARE, IMAGINATION, AND LOVE!

ACKNOWLEDGMENTS

PICTOGRAPHS SHOW THAT FOR MILLENNIA WE HUMANS HAVE IMBUED OUR SHELTERS WITH imagery and design to support our defining values and dreams. Today we are no different—except that the proliferation of publication too often wields a force that would make us wish to be like others instead of ourselves. Therefore, I am most grateful that HarperCollins/Collins Design has decided to publish this book dedicated to those eager to make their homes expressive of their own individual spirit.

The desire of all the people whose homes are shown in the following pages has been to reflect their particular lives, needs and aspirations. By working closely with their architects and designers, they have made sure that their personal environment plays a huge part in their own Manifest Destiny. It is only with their combined understanding that the homes in this book could inspire as they do—each one a salute, not to copying them, but to expressing one's own true self through design. To all I am indebted.

I am also thankful to Marta Schooler at Collins Design for giving me the opportunity to write this book. Marta found me after a long self-imposed hiatus from writing my books about design, asked what I would like to write, and gave me the opportunity to pursue UNIQUE HOMES—an aspect of an idea that I began developing during graduate school. I am thrilled to return to this enlivening voyage to discover new works of enlightenment around the world. In addition, much appreciation is due to Laurie Rippon and Roland Algrant at HarperCollins/Collins Design, for favoring this endeavor.

Most important, it was also Marta Schooler who suggested to George Dick, president of Crescent Hill Books, that he contact me regarding the production of this volume. Since then, guided by Crescent Hills editor Nancy Heinonen, it has been an inspired journey. Thank you, George and Nancy, for your confidence and extraordinary support.

Carol Soucek King

CONTENTS

INTRODUCTION

Do our surroundings really make a difference in how we feel? In the harmony with which we conduct our daily lives? In the exploration of our chosen personal, professional, and spiritual paths? In our physical and mental well-being? In our happiness?

The answer is a resounding "Yes!" Sincerity and a zest for living are the most important qualities, but to reinforce them, they must be given flight on the wings of a personal environment that supports our life quest. They must be allowed to soar with the gently supporting winds of good design, appropriate design, design that states who we really are and helps us be our best. Form, color, texture, light, proportion, and material—as well as cleanliness, order, and understanding—are powerful tools for expressing who we really are. Not primarily for others—although our family and friends will surely benefit from the hospitable and communicative interchange when they experience us in our thoughtfully planned and thought-provoking home—but for ourselves. Good design reverberates, reflects, echoes, and reminds us on a daily basis of our chosen identity, how we wish to spend our hours and who we want to be. Good design is a prayerful expression of our empathy, understanding, and our soul. It helps mold our character. We owe it to ourselves to make the most of every aspect of design in our daily lives. And that is UNIQUE HOMES.

I have come to write this book for the simple reason that I have had to study its subject and have had the opportunity to do so. Through training in theater, design, aesthetics, and communications, I became fascinated by how we see, hear, feel, and express ourselves and how others see, hear, and feel those expressions. Augmented by more than three decades as journalist, editor, and author documenting the work of some of the world's finest shapers of home environments, I have become convinced that design is much more than skin deep; good design is a vital part of our experience on Earth. All that is important in living harmoniously and with individuality must be strived for every day through the spirit of the forms. As we energize our homes with expressions of those attitudes we hold most dear, they will influence our experience and shape our course. They will reinforce who we are and who we want to be.

In design as well as in life, an emphasis on things to the exclusion of values renders all outcomes meaningless. From their first glimpse of where you live, your guests should be given a sense of who you are, not just of what you have. From the moment you awaken, you should surround yourself with sights, textures, sounds, and even fragrances that will uplift your thoughts and add to your appreciation of what you want to come into your life.

We must strive to find what is truly most valuable to each of us as individuals, to commit ourselves to these values, to make them so obvious

that we illuminate our inner selves and reinforce our highest aspirations. When we create our home, we are creating a new universe. Imagine—an untouched, never-before-explored universe! But not in the heavens above—here on Earth! Not of anything pre-existing, but of the explorations of our minds. There is no better place to start than in the home.

Then our homes are not just for ourselves, but also for those we want to have around us. Make your home a haven of comfort and hospitality for all who visit by saying "welcome" from the front door to the garden and every place in between.

Make no mistake: the amount of money that one has and the size of one's home are not factors. Perfect balance has no size. Pleasing proportion has no cost. Cleanliness and order are derived from sensitivity to one's environment, not money; this is true for protective and pleasing placement, and mood-enhancing color and light as well. None of these aspects of good design can be given life without a caring hand and thoughtful eye. The same cannot be said of the well-financed, but insensitive command.

We tune in to never-ending fair winds and gently flowing waters through a sense of life and the power of serenity, so it matters not what your financial situation may be: the best of these creations depend not on money but on soul.

I once knew a designer who had a small apartment and decided to limit herself to seven pieces of furniture. She dwelled in this sparse environment for many years in order to free herself from the need for material accumulation of which she previously experienced in excess and which she had come to find enervating. I would like to add, her apartment was absolutely beautiful.

UNIQUE HOMES is based on dedication, sincerity, and decisiveness. This means fine-tuning on a daily basis and, more often than not, the more pared down and highly edited an environment, the better.

The homes on the following pages were selected not for their reflection of financial good fortune, but for the way they express the nature of those who live within and illuminate their days with surroundings that enrich their souls and enable them to be productive in their chosen paths. These are citadels that extend their inhabitants' thoughts and imaginations, and that make the most of life here on Earth. Their designers have created not only blueprints for houses; they have made blueprints for living.

Remember: your home is *your* personal theater. *You* are the leading character. Your home is the primary place to realize that the world is your stage. Not in any artificial way, but in terms of current function, future dreams and, yes, consideration of others and of the environment. May you make the most of it!
        –Carol Soucek King, M.F.A., Ph.D

A MEDITERRANEAN LOVE AFFAIR

TOP: A reclaimed Chicago brick driveway encircles a Florida live oak, creating a welcome feeling even before one arrives at the one-and-a-half-story mahogany front door. The variously colored tiles of the terra-cotta roof lend a soft, aged appearance to the 1985 Florida Mediterranean house.
RIGHT: Turning the space under the stairway into an intimate retreat at the end of the living room, Jenkins added an antique chaise and covered it with antique gold crushed velvet. The sconce is an antique crystal doré. Additional cushions and small tables make the space user-friendly.

IF THEY HAD HAD THEIR DRUTHERS, THE OWNERS WOULD HAVE transported themselves to the Mediterranean in a minute. Now they don't have to.

Drawn to the style of this home, which indeed is known locally as Miami Mediterranean, they snatched it up at the first opportunity and, with designer **Dennis Jenkins**, further emphasized its character by adding the colors, textures, and feelings of their beloved Tuscany, Provence, and a few other favorite spots in Italy and France.

It is a perfect match for this couple and their grown children, whose lifestyle reflects the casual familial way they associate with their favorite European ports of call. They practically live on the porch out back, gathering friends and family around their old Italian farmhouse table and a mixture of other pieces they have picked up here and there. Nothing seems especially designed and much of it is not—but everything seems cherished—a tribute to the caring owners and a triumph for Jenkins, who actually did specify or custom design many of the home's furnishings.

Another favorite gathering place is the kitchen with its cantaloupe-colored Venetian plaster walls, their hue and texture similar to walls that dazzled one of the owners when visiting Portofino. They reflect her idea that everything to do with food should feed the spirit as well—set it soaring with plenty of laughter and warmth. To her even the cooking itself should be a shared experience, and she likes everyone in the house to join her as she expertly chops, tosses, and mixes one of her favorite dishes at her large prep island. Apropos is the dress in this comfortable environment: even for entertaining, it is always blue jeans.

She says she is not a crystal kind of girl, so she felt free to express her imagination along with Jenkins in substituting traditional amenities with touches throughout the home, continuing the feeling of joie de vivre. Together they came up with the idea of the checkerboard detail on the dining room ceiling, similar to a detail Jenkins has in his own home in nearby Coconut Grove. What was her inspiration for a daughter's bedroom with its hues of blue, yellow, lilac, and cream along with its faux fireplace? Once again—a visit to a favorite European destination, Claude Monet's home and gardens at Giverny.

MIAMI, FLORIDA

PHOTOGRAPHY BY LANNY PROVO

LEFT: The dining room's enveloping warmth is created by numerous aspects, most notably the walls plastered in a rich garnet Venetian stucco and an antique chandelier selected by the owners at Marvin Alexander in New York City. To encourage conversation to continue long after dessert, Dennis Jenkins designed the dining chairs covered in a rich silk/viscose/polyester blend with comfort in mind. The ceiling's checkerboard detail designed by Dennis Jenkins was executed by local faux artist Ann Yonover.

TOP AND RIGHT: Venetian stucco in a melon hue and waxed to a moderate sheen emphasizes the owners' wish to make the kitchen a jovial gathering place. The addition of trim molding brings interest to the ceiling. The flooring is the same beige travertine that flows throughout the home's entire ground level, save for the master bedroom. All countertops are granite. The breakfast chairs are French country and were hand painted by faux artist Ellen Moss.

TOP: Besides the kitchen, the covered porch is where this family mostly lives —gathered around the old Italian farmhouse table amid the lush garden. The eclectic furnishings include Thai teak furniture, an old rice container for additional seating and storage, and silk throw pillows made from fabric salvaged from an antique spread. Hanging light fixtures that hold candles break up the vertical plane and, with the antique iron candle stands, lend evening hours a romantic, mellow glow. A gilt-framed mirror adds to the feeling of the indoor/outdoor space and makes the columns appear to continue to infinity. The simulated keystone flooring and columns existed when the house was purchased.

RIGHT: To heighten the elegance of a small powder room, Jenkins duplicated the exterior simulated stone of the quatrefoil window on the interior and increased the size of the baseboard. The walls are painted warm ochre to enhance the room's array of golden accents, including a custom-framed gold-flecked antique mirror and the Art Nouveau doré chandelier with six Favrile Glass shades.

TOP, LEFT, AND RIGHT: The Impressionistic colors of a daughter's bedroom were inspired by the clients' admiration for Claude Monet's home in Giverny, with faux artist Ellen Moss carrying the hues of the fabrics to the walls, crown moldings, cornices, and furniture. By staining and hand rubbing, she gave the periwinkle blue table a particularly distressed, aged appearance. For the faux fireplace, a wood construction designed by Dennis Jenkins, she simulated lapis lazuli. The floor is French pine. The vanilla-colored sheers have over drapes of blue and yellow stripes, which have been hung horizontally over the balcony doors, vertically at the windows. Lolling on a chair is the family member Dasher, an energetic Jack Russell.

IN CONCERT WITH THE GREAT OUTDOORS

TOP: The details of the entry vestibule's merchant tansu [c.1890] and Niermann Weeks mirror immediately express the architect's subtle Arts & Crafts theme. All wood trim is Douglas fir and ties in nicely to the exterior and surroundings with its natural finish. Beaunotte limestone floor tiles are from Clovis Collection. The two photographs hanging in the stairwell leading down to the kitchen are "Floating Nude" by Edward Weston and "Dogwood Blossoms" by Ansel Adams.

RIGHT: The kitchen is designed so that the home owner and friends can be seated during informal dining service at the John Hall cherry wood Regency-style dining table (with fireplace behind, not shown). For more formal affairs, the John Hall table in the living room is pulled out toward the staircase landing in an area where the lighting designer has placed ceiling lights to focus on the table when used for dining there.

THIS HARMONIOUS MARRIAGE OF EARTHINESS AND SOPHISTICATION WAS created for a gentleman who appreciates the great outdoors as much as he appreciates a fine concert hall. Located in the forest on California's central coast and designed by **David Allen Smith Architect, Yoko Whitaker/Whitaker & Phillips Decoration,** and **Linda Ferry Lighting Design**, his home echoes the area's prevalent influence of the Arts & Crafts tradition with classic modern elements.

The entry's Beaunotte limestone floor tiles continue down the hall into the study and into the kitchen, commencing the flow from the exterior's redwood shingles washed to blend in with the surrounding trees, and move harmoniously to the interior's cherry wood cabinets and color-integrated plaster walls. Jean Michel Frank and Mies van der Rohe designs mesh well here with Japanese tansu and Tibetan rugs, and harmonize with old timber pine floors, French limestone fireplaces, natural Douglas fir trim work, natural redwood doors, handmade ceramic tiles, and the brushed steel/white bronze and brushed nickel hardware throughout.

Hues of the surrounding nature were brought inside with a calm palette of sand, toast, camel, honey, sage, moss, and pale olive punctuated by an occasional dash of pomegranate red. With the living room's tall, unadorned windows on either side, one feels as if one is in the midst of the forest itself.

Understated lighting complements the delicate sylvan touch, already augmented by the architect's provision for multiple skylights, bay windows, and floor-to-ceiling windows placed to capture the capricious daylight of a forest setting. The architecture of the exposed structure required careful placement and a minimum of surface-mounted light fixtures, while the widely varying ceiling heights demanded a different lighting solution for each room.

Upon entering this home, one is in a subtle world that envelops and draws one in gently. Nothing overwhelms. Instead, the attention is to the detail, the clean lines, the amazement that absolutely nothing is superfluous, like the inexplicable poetry of a symphony.

CARMEL, CALIFORNIA

PHOTOGRAPHY BY RUSSELL MACMASTERS PHOTOGRAPHY

TOP: The living room combines classic modern elements, particularly in the upholstery from Donghia and Christian Liaigre, with Arts & Crafts. Included are Sloan Miyasato's Cole Porter chairs, Murray's Iron Works' Weaved Iron Coffee Table, Macassar ebony floor lamps from Rose Tarlow, Baker Knapp & Tubbs's lacquered coffee table by Barbara Barry. Above the fireplace is "Carmel River Estuary" by Edward Bruce (1879-1943), oil on canvas. The area rug is Tufenkian, from Tibet.

LEFT: In this house, placing the piano away from traffic and surrounded by the view seemed preferable to sequestering it from weather and light, as is traditional. A Rodney Hunter Collection hand carved vintage Indonesian teak settee and The McGuire Furniture Co. teak lounge chairs are on the deck.

RIGHT: A northern Italian style library/dining table by John Hall, set with Murano glass lamps and cymbidium orchids in a vintage basket from the Philippines, welcomes guests into the living room with its fireplace beyond. The vertical steel ribbons of the sound system on either side of the fireplace have been carefully integrated with the design palette. Roy Lichtenstein's untitled brass head sculpture (1970) rests on a cherry wood pedestal. The interior designer worked hand-in-hand with the lighting designer, as the electrical work is one of the first things that has to be planned, yet cannot be done without a final furniture plan from the interior designer.

LEFT: Continuing the interconnected feeling of craftsmanship in the master bedroom, the designer counterpoised a Japanese gentleman's tansu [c. 1870] with Arts & Crafts as well as classic modern. Included are a Tibetan area rug from Tufenkian, a walnut sleigh bed from Dessin Fournir, Rogers & Goffigon alpaca and wool coverlet with Anachini cotton pillow shams. Over the bed is Michael Kainer's "George Washington Park," oil on canvas, and next to it is Erlinda Hiscock's untitled Big Sur landscape. Above the tansu are two photographs [1962 and 1967] by Ruth Bernhard.

TOP: The master bath is sheathed in a golden cream-colored French lime-stone that provides a soothing and neutral setting ideal for grooming and dressing. The stool is from Todd Hase and the Tibetan rug from Endless Knot is woven with a water pattern.

RIGHT: Even the powder room has a masculine tone with its clean lines, and lack of superfluous details. The bachelor client wanted the feeling of the nearby Big Sur country, understated earthiness, yet also elegance and refinement. Waterworks satin nickel wash stand with Beaunotte limestone top and Morrison brushed nickel sconces. The walnut and silver-leaf framed mirror is from Michael Berman.

HOLLYWOOD'S GOLDEN AGE

FROM HER END OF THE FILM BUSINESS, SHE EXUDES FLAIR AND creativity; he does the same in his world of investments. They both deeply appreciate having the opportunity to be part of a world steeped in romance—the world of old Hollywood.

When this couple came upon one particular 1927 Spanish-style home in a historic part of the Hollywood Hills, they were drawn instantly to its unique legacy—the location for the Raymond Chandler/Billy Wilder screenplay classic noir film, *Double Indemnity*, nominated for seven Academy Awards. Equally compelling, the home could meet the couple's personal needs—a comfortable retreat at the end of busy professional days as well as a place where they could entertain friends for casual dinners or have larger parties spilling out onto the patio.

Although many of the original details were still intact, it was the task of interior designer **Mae Brunken**, **Mae Brunken Design**, to bring the rest of the house back to its original period elegance, largely undoing an unfortunate 1970s remodel. In the process, many jewels of the original house revealed themselves, ready to be refinished and restored. Others had to be re-created.

Hardwood floors and tile were uncovered, refinished, and restored. Door hardware, fixtures, and lighting that had been switched over the years were replaced with period pieces. Wood beams, some of which had been painted vivid white, were sanded and stained. In addition, the ceiling overlooking the entry was hand-stenciled by decorative artist Leesa Martling.

In the courtyard, a twelve-person whirlpool was replaced with a pergola for more versatile outdoor living and a fountain fashioned from treasured Malibu tile. Used bricks were laid with sand for the hardscape, and Mexican tile insets were installed on stair risers. Bringing it all back to life was garden designer **Lisa Moseley**.

A mix of both modern and antique pieces and a current color palette infused with references to the vibrant Art Deco era salute this particular couple's eclectic taste, strong sense of style, and their goal to infuse their home with the flair of old Hollywood glamour.

TOP: The intimate nature of the house is captured by the stunning fireplace, which was replaced by the previous owner due to earthquake damage. Partnered with a Quan Yin sculpture, the Ethel Erlandson Glover painting rests on the wood mantel. The vintage antique store-find fireplace screen sets off the striking modernist coffee table that holds a personal vase collection featuring an alabaster urn and Murano glass bowl.

RIGHT: The owners' marble-and-stone pedestal dining table is combined with Spanish Colonial leather chairs and tempered by a romantic crystal chandelier. An antique textile rests on the table, while the artwork is by a friend of the owners. A hand-carved wooden mirror above the buffet is flanked by mismatched nineteenth century Italian high-backed armchairs.

LOS ANGELES, CALIFORNIA

PHOTOGRAPHY BY ROBERT BERGER, BERGER/CONSER PHOTOGRAPHY

FIRST FLOOR PLAN

SECOND FLOOR PLAN

RIGHT: Perfect for summertime naps, this vintage iron daybed is shaded by the pergola and piled high with a bevy of sensuously hued pillows. The Etrusche-style lounge chair works to create an intimate conversation area. A vintage textile accentuates the carved wooden coffee table. Bravely surrounded by wicker chairs is the custom-designed concrete-and-tile dining table, perfect for lounging after al fresco meals. The exterior stays true to the 1920s style. OPPOSITE PAGE: Coppery silk drapery edged with a single band of pink creates a strong vertical element that helps to balance the beamed ceiling and softly framed upholstered pieces. The sofa is covered in a rich cocoa-brown velvet and the chairs in pink with brown piping, all residing on a contemporary rug that grounds the room with its strong graphic pattern. The Madonna, purchased at auction through Christie's, hangs over a 1930s deco bar adjacent to the game table (not shown).

LEFT: The palette in the master bedroom was chosen to be sexy, soft, and romantic. It is reminiscent of the Art Deco period. The area rug is custom and was modified from a vintage pattern. Ivory silk curtains further soften the room and block out light. The chair is French Deco, and the antique armoire belonged to the client.

TOP: The original banister and fixture grace the scene where Barbara Stanwyck walks down the original Malibu-tiled staircase in the film *Double Indemnity*. Movie posters, including one resting on the antique coffer, are part of the clients' personal film noir collection. The figure in the foreground is a Peruvian artifact.

TOP RIGHT: As part of the restoration, the 1920s style hand-painted-and-stenciled ceiling works to cap the red tile floor. The ceiling's intriguing pattern was adapted from the wrought iron railing. The unique round windows are original to the house.

RIGHT: Central to the rest of the home, the library offers a fine reading area, with built-in bookcases (not shown), while the leather chaise and ottoman have become the favorite place to unwind at day's end. The shag rug further enhances the coziness of the space, while the linen roman shade blocks out late afternoon sun. Vintage pottery rests in what was once the telephone niche. The lamp was the clients' own, and dwells on an Art Deco side table.

AMERICAN ARTIST, PAINTER, AND SCULPTOR JOSEPH SHEPPARD purchased this formerly derelict 300-year-old farmhouse near Pietrasanta, Italy, the epicenter for artists worldwide, even before interior designer **Rita St. Clair** had entered the picture. Soon after his beginnings at restoration, the interior was enhanced by St. Clair's high-style expertise, which was then tempered by the sublimity of the cypress- and blossom-filled Tuscan countryside.

From the verdant terrace to the kitchen gathering place and its surrounding rooms, to the outbuildings of Joe's studios and their frequent guests, all spell h-o-m-e. Sheppard spends most of the year in Italy, and St. Clair's year is mostly in Baltimore, Maryland, her home office, but she continues to work in Italy in the summer and fall on interior design commissions and writing her syndicated column "Design Line." She believes that Italy is the ideal place for an inspirational getaway as well as the place to both find and design upscale furnishings for international interior design projects.

A Guggenheim Foundation Grant enabled Sheppard to develop his skills in painting and figurative art in Florence, many years before acquiring this farmhouse. However, Italy is as much home to him as Maryland, where he was born to a farming family.

The result of Joe and Rita's joint efforts is quite evident. Their respect for the vernacular architecture, at the same time providing space for their creativity and lifestyle and the display of Sheppard's works, is a salute to integrity toward the spirit of place as much as it is to self-expression.

The outside of the buildings is washed with a subtle apricot color, while the walls inside are all white to brighten the interior as well as allow Sheppard's paintings and sculptures to stand as counterpoints.

On the second floor, a few skylights were added to allow more daylight—a difficult addition, since Italian laws governing the renovation of what are considered historic houses allow few alterations to the facade or footprint. This home still feels like an original farmhouse, where the animals were housed on the first floor providing warmth for the farmers living above them, at a time when people lived close to the land.

TOP AND RIGHT: A sculpture garden and olive grove provide entry to the Sheppard/St. Clair Italian home, a typical Tuscan farmhouse that housed animals and farmhands. The structure of stone, rubble, and cement has been rehabilitated without losing its original character. Flanking the main house and terrace is a stone wall with Sheppard's rendition of a grotesque mask, which serves as a mail slot.

PIETRASANTA, ITALY

PHOTOGRAPHY COURTESY OF RITA ST. CLAIR ASSOCIATES

TOP LEFT AND TOP RIGHT: The door from the kitchen to the pantry was formerly plastered over. The exposed brick is the opening for the storage area below the original outside stairway to the farmers living quarters, discovered only during the renovation. The oven, four-burner cooktop, and sink area are either sunken beneath or placed on top of one local slab of white marble, now properly stained by good food and cooking. Rita St. Clair finds this ample space and equipment for cooking for twenty or more guests. The couple found the multicolored rustic tiles in Sicily, not typical of the more subdued ceramics of Tuscany, but more expressive of their own more exotic tastes. The decorative tile inserts that appear as decorative fruit plates were handmade and painted to their request by Falsini, a ceramicist in Florence.

LEFT: The dining area of the terrace overlooking mountains and a valley is the place for everyday dining and entertaining. It is a good place to read a book and relax.

RIGHT: A walk off the terrace leads directly into the kitchen. This makes serving easy and food preparation fun for Rita, who likes to prepare food for friends and family. The kitchen is used for old-fashioned cooking—no dishwasher, no microwave, no garbage disposal—but a big refrigerator and a generous pantry, which are always filled with treasures from the vegetable garden and olive grove. An antique farmer's table and a painted buffet are overseen by a copper-hooded light fixture. Half of the kitchen is barely 8 feet in height. Above it is an open loft— the master bedroom, which overlooks the rest of the kitchen and soars upward two stories to the original timbered ceiling.

TOP: On the opposite wall of Rita St. Clair's home office and sitting room, an array of white canvas slipcovers plays down the richness of the dark chestnut wood furniture from the region and serves as counterpoint to the couple's colorful international collection.

TOP RIGHT: The room located off a spiral staircase and next to Sheppard's portrait painting studio has become a family room for watching television and lighting a fire in the only remaining fireplace in the house. The rug is an antique Heriz.

RIGHT: The fireplace original to the farmhouse in Rita St. Clair's home office in Italy is surrounded by her collection of antique farmhouse plates and ceramics—not fine plates, but those she collects at open air markets for her collection of countryware.

OPPOSITE PAGE: In the living room, we find an antique desk covered with family pictures. As in the rest of the house, all seating is covered in white canvas, the woodwork is dark chestnut, the walls are white, the floors are the original terra cotta tiles, and the rugs are antique and decorative. The living room's rug is an antique Kilim.

FULL BOUNTY

TOP: The dining room's predominant deep red sets off the room's polished wood, including the monastery table and French carved coffer, and is reiterated in the tapestry pattern of the upholstered dining chairs. The room also has brass chateau candlesticks, a Russian icon that once hung in a church alcove, and red Dupioni silk drapery with gold banding frames the garden beyond.

RIGHT: The living room's design was spun off of the untitled triptych of Easter Island by Dorothy Preston. Tabriz area rug. There is a custom silk-covered club chair, damask sofa, custom pillows with antique trim, and a cabriole leg ebony-and-glass coffee table. The chaise rests beside the fireplace (not seen), which is flanked by bookcases filled with a combination of the Jennisons' favorite authors and leather-bound books.

LIVING AT THE BEACH WHILE THEIR CHILDREN GREW UP, WES AND Beth Jennison recently found themselves ready for a house in the city. The home with which they fell in love offered both a desirable location convenient to all of their favorite shops and restaurants and a unique, spacious dwelling to entertain friends and family, and also house their remarkable collections.

As the Senior Vice President of UBS Financial Services, a wife who has devoted herself to charitable community services, and two daughters bringing college friends home, the Jennisons have created a bountiful life and live it fully in their home. They sought out **Mae Brunken Design** to create the ideal environment that would truly fit their new lifestyle—casual elegance with eclectic flair.

Since the house was newly built, only minor renovations took place. The first change was to re-create the existing housekeeper's quarters into a wine cellar able to house Mr. Jennison's 3,000-plus-bottle wine collection. Prior to the cellar, the wine had to be stored in multiple lockers around town. Another change involved relocating or removing various air ducts and niches in the living room so that a large triptych painting could finally be hung as one piece (in prior residences, it had always been split into three different locations). In addition, a gym was added to provide Mrs. Jennison, an avid runner, with a place to work out on non-running days. Finally, the room that has proven to be the ultimate hub of the house, the redesigned gourmet kitchen is now able to handle the constant flow of guests that spill over from the dining room.

With Mr. Jennison's mother and a family friend as artists, as well as having added to their collection on their travels, colors were often suggested by these possessions as well as by good psychology. For example, the earthy tones of the triptych set off a succession of relaxed, neutral hues in the living room, and the rich ruby tones in a Russian icon placed in the dining room are picked up in the walls' deep resonant red that also enhances the dinner table's lively atmosphere.

At day's end, the Jennisons sleep in a carved four-poster bed that belonged to his mother as a child, and which Brunken had enlarged. The three additional bedrooms are reserved for the Jennisons' daughters and frequent overnight guests.

SANTA MONICA, CALIFORNIA

PHOTOGRAPHY BY ROBERT BERGER, BERGER/CONSER PHOTOGRAPHY

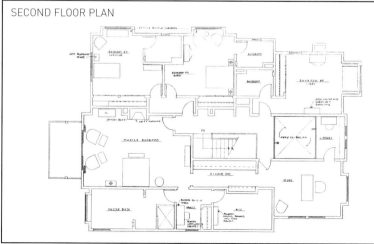

SECOND FLOOR PLAN

TOP: The full-size sentimental bed was taken to a craftsman specializing in antique restoration. There, by duplicating the existing carving and dowelling flawlessly, the bed was enlarged to a king size, which matches the master bedroom's large scale. It faces a fireplace (not shown) and is flanked by a pair of mismatched Italian chests of drawers used as nightstands. The painted and gilded hand-turned lamps, damask fabric on the club chairs and ottomans, and crewel embroidered drapery serve as light counterpoints to the deep olive of the custom-made bedding.

RIGHT: For this most informal area, the family room's tufted leather ottoman works as both coffee table and footstool—both necessities while watching a movie. To that end (but not shown), a flat-screen television was mounted above the fireplace and encircled by artwork. The Jennisons' own sofa has been slipcovered in mink-colored velvet and strewn with custom throw pillows in hand-washed velvets with antique trims. A fur throw adds a welcome touch to the leather club chair. The room is lit by French polished cone lamps. Belgian linen drapery blocks out daylight when necessary for television viewing or opens for a view of the pool.

PARADISE AT HOME

TOP: The home is located in a historic villa's greenhouse, transformed into a residence. Cibic added awnings to create a feeling of greater depth to the interior.

RIGHT: The living area shows many pieces designed by Aldo Cibic during his Standard period, when he wished to express a respect for the past and its ancestral leanings. Instead of making unique objects with strong personalities, he was drawn to quality furnishings for everyday life: "normale con brio." Thus the slipcovered white sofa in the living room is strictly Standard and reflecting the same philosophy is the coffee table. The six abstract paintings are by Erin Sharp. Keith Haring created the inflatable animal sculpture.

EVERY TIME ITALIAN ARCHITECT **ALDO CIBIC, CIBIC & PARTNERS**, MOVES, it becomes a chance for him to better realize who he is. He has had numerous homes in many different places, each one expressing what and who he was at that exact moment of his life. The house in which he lives now is the greenhouse of a Palladian villa and it truly speaks to him and his family and how they wish to live.

For example, there is the style—or non-style—just a space expressing vitality to him, his family, and his associates whom he frequently invites over for what become all-night discussions. To him, home is a matter of adjusting a place and enriching it with the passing of time. To him, art is the domestication of a space, the gradual process of rendering a house welcoming and full of life. So it is not surprising that every piece of furniture has a story.

For example, one of Cibic's most unusual pieces is an elephant made of net usually used for rabbit cages. He treasures it, particularly as it was made by his friend, the artist Benedetta Mori Ubaldini.

Yet most of the furniture here has been designed by Cibic himself, renowned for decades for his involvement with the Memphis Movement and then establishing his own Standard Period aesthetic (1990-1991). He says his designs represent the different periods in his life, and that he commissions other pieces just to achieve his dreams.

Cibic's favorite place is the bedroom. He spends long hours there, many of them surrounded by family, others happily alone with his books, bathtub, and television. The living room is also an important space for him—originally a stable, now furnished casually, with an assortment of his own designs. Within the same vaulted ceiling is the dining space—where he usually plays with his son Jan.

Cibic also adores the kitchen—expansively welcoming and made of inexpensive materials and furnishings. The fireplace was pre-existing, as was an old marble basin.

One can sense Cibic's enjoyment in combining colors, art, strange forms, and beloved objects to create energy, vitality, and happiness throughout the house.

VICENZA, ITALY

PHOTOGRAPHY BY SANTI CALECA

TOP AND FAR LEFT: The bedroom and bath overlook the living area and provide plenty of space for Cibic's constantly growing collection of books on the floor, around the tub, and in the newly added shelves. All wood is pine. Throughout the house, natural linen and dark green velvet continue the window covering. Perhaps more than any other place, his personal retreat spells home for this intellectual explorer—a symbol of Cibic's vision of surrounding oneself not so much with style, but with a feeling of warm and pleasing functionality.

LEFT: The dining room's painted wood chairs and table (now produced by A&P Contract) are from Aldo Cibic's Standard period, when he longed to express distinct architectonic forms around which items for living could be gathered. His aim has not been mass production, but the definition of a personal standard in the sense of taking care of oneself— meaning to surround oneself with objects that would stand out not because of style, but because of their warm, pleasant, functional quality. The white and glass cabinet, designed by Cibic and produced by F.lli Boffi, Lentate s/S, holds a collection of citron bottles. The table lamp is from Habitat. The blue straw rug is from India. The glass and steel dividing wall is original to the house.

TOP: In the kitchen, Vicenza stone on the counter is overseen by green resin on the splash wall. Cibic designed the shelf above the wall in pinewood as used in the room's original ceiling.
RIGHT: Aldo Cibic had always dreamed about an animal sculpture in his house, and when his friend Federica Mori Ubaldini started to create such figures in net usually used for rabbit cages, he asked her to make one for him. Thus Cibic's elephant sculpture was born.

ART-FILLED URBANITY

TOP: Presenting a fine welcome—the home's original Victorian fencing and the owners' dog.

RIGHT: Comfortable seating beckons in the library/study/media room with its deep, custom made sofas and armchair covered in a Stroheim & Romann deep teal chenille. The walls are covered in a silken grass cloth. The large painting is "Burning Ropes" by Tim Storrier. Floors throughout this area were replaced with recycled timber made from indigenous Australian eucalyptus trees. The rug is antique Persian.

BEING SITUATED IN A CHARMING INNER CITY SUBURB THAT IS THE center of Sydney's café society makes this home ideal for its owners, a successful businessman and his artist wife, as they frequent the area's theater, opera, and galleries regularly. It is nearby their family, grandchild, and many friends, a factor along with the owners' generous hospitality that regularly sets this late Victorian double terrace residence (two terrace houses consolidated into one) humming with both informal and formal gatherings. It is not so large as to inhibit their desire to travel, which they do extensively.

When they first spoke to their longtime designer **Meryl Hare**, **Hare & Klein Pty Ltd**, about this—the twelfth project she has done for them—they said they wanted it to reflect their relaxed lifestyle. They also hoped it would show their substantial art collection to its best advantage, have something of a "wow" factor without inhibiting a small child, and above all, be comfortable.

Extensive renovations were done to make the two terraces and the two main reception rooms on one level so they could connect—necessitating lowering the floor of one and dismantling, then later reinstating, the two fireplaces. Paneling was installed to line up with the windows, thus maintaining the rooms' proportions.

The newly adjoining entry and living rooms were opened up to increase circulation space without compromising any of the original features. Since this side of the house gets little natural light, the area is treated as an evening sitting room. The back of the house was extensively remodeled, with a family/dining room opened on one side to the kitchen and on the other side to a private courtyard with a lap pool. Upstairs, one bedroom was converted into a dressing room with a bathroom connected to another to comprise the master suite. Another is used as a gym, and a third doubles as a guest room and artist's studio.

Throughout, a relaxed, yet highly urbane, environment expresses the clients' interests and personalities, yet the entirety of this scintillating compendium of rooms is compact enough for them to close up and journey onward.

SYDNEY, AUSTRALIA

PHOTOGRAPHY BY MARK GREEN

LEFT: An antique Chinese console supporting a Robert Kuo Cloud lamp hand finished in silver plate serves as a gentle divider between reception and seating areas.

RIGHT: This is the first view of the interior from the home's entry. To answer the clients' wish for dramatic impact here, Meryl Hare used a bold color combination including the dark stucco applied to the walls, which were then highly waxed, giving them a reflective quality. Sheer silk for the generous curtains allows daylight in while providing privacy from the street. The deep red rug designed by Hare + Klein is custom made in a combination of wool and silk by Tibetan weavers. An antique circular chinoiserie table is accompanied by a chaise covered in Thai silk in front of the fireplace— a quiet place to read. The painting above the mantel is by Australian artist Arthur Boyd, whose family once owned this house.

TOP LEFT: Although the reception room and seating area beyond were opened up by removing sections of walls, all the original late Victorian features were retained. It is interesting to note that, though the walls in these two connected rooms are dark, their waxed reflectivity makes the quality of light good both day and night. The lighting fixtures in both rooms were custom made for this project. The painting in the seating area is by Australian artist John Olsen.

TOP: The sofa was rescued from the clients' previous home. The scatter cushions were made from fragments of old African textiles, and the beaded headrest on the coffee table is from the Ivory Coast.

LEFT: As the floor in the library/study/media room was lowered to connect to the reception/seating rooms, the position of the windows is higher than originally intended. To compensate and also lend a warm atmosphere, the joinery timber was continued through the room in paneling. The plasma television screen is incorporated into the joinery, with the facility of a large screen and projector concealed within the ceiling.

RIGHT: The master bedroom's walls are covered with a silk finish grass cloth in a light taupe, bringing a romantic softness to the room without making it too feminine. The armchair, one of several items rescued from a previous home, is upholstered in a Stroheim & Romann silk velvet. The bed is dressed in soft chenille and silk.

SIMPLY MARVELOUS

TOP AND RIGHT: From the entry located on the upper level, steps descend to the living room with its ceiling at a soaring 11-foot 3-inch height and view of the Sonoma Valley below. The two chaises with plywood frames were designed by Marcel Breuer, with whom Abercrombie once practiced, and are upholstered with Gretchen Bellinger fabric. The checkerboard-patterned rug is from Peru.

STANLEY ABERCROMBIE AND **PAUL VIEYRA** DIDN'T WANT MUCH, JUST the best: a relatively small 2,400-square-foot, no-frills space, but with superb function, materials, lighting by **Susan Brady**, and with furnishings by some of the twentieth century's most renowned designers who were, as are these two architects, devoted Modernists. The ceilings commence at 9-feet 3-inches and soar upward over the entirety of the structure's major portion to 11-feet 3-inches.

They owned their land overlooking prime wine country scenery for years before moving from New York City. Design critic/author Abercrombie was *Interior Design* magazine's longtime editor-in-chief, and Vieyra a prominent figure at Skidmore, Owings & Merrill and later at Gensler.

For the massive 18-inch-thick walls, they selected Ener-Grid blocks made of recycled polystyrene and Portland cement, completely fireproof as is fitting in this fire-hazardous area. The walls are finished inside and out with earth from a local quarry. Aesthetically, its rough texture and rich earthy color derived directly from the quarry's soil make the house a reflection of its natural environment.

The house seems twice its actual size due to the openness of its design. It includes no hallways. Doorways are aligned so as to provide direct views from one end to the other and beyond through many windows. Adding to the airiness is a skylight running the entire 36-foot length of the living room. Save for some ingeniously flexible floor lamps by the masterful Cedric Hartman, space-consuming items such as table lamps and freestanding cabinetry have been avoided. Instead, most of the interior walls have been fitted with open bookshelves based on the building blocks' 15-inch module to preserve continuity of proportion. All other dividing partitions are sand-colored laminate and serve as storage. For a change of pace, the living room's fireplace wall is faced with perforated aluminum tiles, and sliding doors and kitchen backsplash add an occasional burst of color.

Abercrombie and Vieyra find they can continue their writing and architectural projects in Sonoma just as well as they could in Manhattan. And here they have room for something more—a separate art studio so that Abercrombie can also delve into his passion for painting without cluttering their new home's pared-down, but not so simple simplicity.

SONOMA, CALIFORNIA

PHOTOGRAPHY BY PETER PAIGE

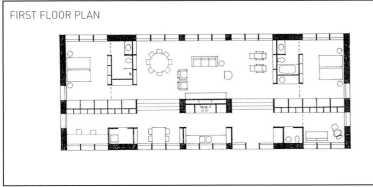

FIRST FLOOR PLAN

TOP: The great sweep of the living room is kept free of clutter, including window coverings that were deemed unnecessary except in the two bedrooms. Interest is brought to the high ceiling through tongue-and-groove redwood planks recovered from an Oakland waterfront factory when demolished. Many pieces are gifts or designed by Abercrombie and Vieyra's personal friends: the large brown rug traversed with thin markings is from Egypt and was a gift from the late Edgar Kaufmann, Jr., once design curator of the Museum of Modern Art in New York City; the red leather chair is by friend Mario Bellini; chairs by another friend, Mario Botta, who designed the Museum of Modern Art in San Francisco, are gathered around the circular concrete dining table of Abercrombie and Vieyra's own design. The three lithographs hanging in front of the far bookshelves are by Robert Rauschenberg. The woman by the poolside is a sculpture by James Mason.

TOP LEFT AND RIGHT: The two bedrooms at either end of the symmetrical floor plan open to the pool and provide ample closet space behind the modular floor-to-ceiling closets faced with sand-colored laminate. The twin beds in both rooms have vertical headboards covered with silk from Barbara Beckmann Studios and bedspreads of Gretchen Bellinger fabric. For light control, Mecho shades provide this completely private home's only window treatment. The sculpture is an ancestor effigy by the Giriama people of Kenya.
RIGHT: The kitchen's backsplash is made of two pieces of laminated glass painted an earthy green in between to provide a note of color.

TRAVELS AND MEMORIES

TOP: Having arrived to the entry in the inclinator, guests proceed along the steps over a koi pond toward the level area, which leads to the front door—an old pair of Rajasthan doors, joined. The totems at right are house posts from Mali in West Africa and at night they cast wonderful shadows.

RIGHT: The entry vestibule has a wall deliberately interrupting the view to the water. The painting is one in a series by Katherine Boland. On the left the Indian temple columns define the entry to the media area. On the right is a large antique sideboard from the north of China and, in the distance to the left, is a painting by South African artist Margaret Forster.

INTERIOR DESIGNER **MERYL HARE**, **HARE & KLEIN PTY LTD**, AND HER husband purchased this waterfront home on Sydney's Middle Harbour in the early 1990s. They knew it would be a longtime work-in-progress, especially as it is located on an extremely steep site with access only from an inclinator—a lift device that moves up and down the slope on a rail.

At first they viewed the access as a problem, but soon became accustomed to the unusual mode of transport and appreciated the beauty of the journey and the privacy it afforded. The couple and their two daughters were sure to remember their school lunches as the journey both ways takes about five minutes—forever if you are late!

They started their series of renovations and rebuilding from the bottom up. First was the swimming pool, while their daughters were still young enough to enjoy it. Next came remodeling the home's two lower levels with a view to the final stage involving the demolition of the top level and rebuilding. Construction was difficult because of the access; building materials sometimes had to be moved by barge, which periodically became grounded during low tide. Nonetheless, the family staged the building so that at all times they could live on site, supervise, and enjoy. Although this all sounds tedious, the family had a vision of what they wanted, and to them, the astoundingly scenic location made up for the hardship.

The Hares' daughters have left home, so while the house is larger than one couple needs, they often have visitors and enjoy entertaining. Overall, their lifestyle is casual and relaxed. For Meryl Hare, her home is a refuge from her work, a place to recharge. It is also an expression of personal taste and comfort. Meryl Hare and her husband have collected artifacts and art during many years and many journeys and treasure each piece. The aesthetics of their home give this couple endless pleasure.

SYDNEY, AUSTRALIA

PHOTOGRAPHY BY JENNIFER HARE

TOP LEFT: The living room's seating area has two very deep sofas, which are especially comfortable for tall people. Three of the scatter cushions are made from African Kuba cloth fragments and one from Italian silk velvet. The sofa is flanked by two kimono chests and the windows behind, which let in the north light—important to those living in the southern hemisphere—are dressed with simple matchstick blinds, stained chocolate. The coffee tables are a constantly changing landscape of favorite objects, books, flowers and, of course—coffee!

TOP RIGHT: In the corner of the living room: a black lacquered kimono chest, one of a pair that Meryl Hare acquired many years ago; the painting above is by Australian artist Katherine Boland and was inspired by the bush fires the country experienced during the 1990s; a horse that is an antique Guatemalan child's toy; and behind it is an old Vietnamese bowl, again collected on a trip. The West African anklet and bracelets are part of a larger collection and are very old.

LEFT: The guest suite is the only accommodation on the top level, so it is quite private. The black lacquered bedside cabinets are Chinese. The couple purchased the painting on a trip to Vietnam. The bedcover is Indian.

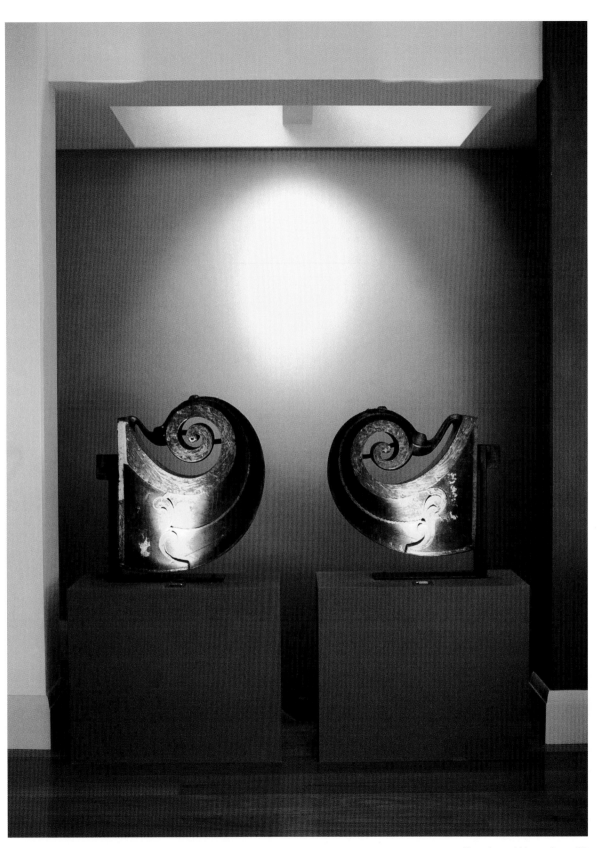

TOP: This detail of the guest powder room is of the West African timber bowl, which Hare adapted to a wash hand-basin. It is mounted on a slab of Spanish Black Limestone and the wall behind is painted in a deep pepper lime-wash color.

RIGHT: The plinths with recessed up-lights have boat prows mounted on them and obviate the need for a balustrade. Meryl Hare purchased these years ago, without understanding exactly what they were. Later, she and her husband traveled through Kerala in the south of India and realized that they were typical of the boat prows of this region. These are obviously antiques, but the modern ones, very much in use, are a similar size and shape.

PAST AND PRESENT

TOP: Shapiro credits his personal style to his extensive travels in Europe and visits to homes of major collectors. He says he soaked up the European approach to design, the casual treatment of great objects, a nonchalance toward mixing a wide variety of seemingly disparate elements and styles, and the importance placed on antiquity, patina, and classical references. Here in his entry hall, he juxtaposes Ellsworth Kelly's "Black Curve" with a first-century Roman marble torso of an Amazon warrior. The floor is pillow-cut, closely abutted limestone. The iron balustrade was original to the house.

RIGHT: At the stairwell balcony overlooking the front entry, from left to right: James Casebere's photograph of Monticello; a seventeenth-century Italian sculpture of Mary Magdalene; a two-part wall drawing by Mel Bochner (conceived in the 1960s and executed by the artist directly on the wall in 2000); and, below, an early (1961) John Chamberlain sculpture, "Bijou."

THROUGHOUT EVERY ROOM IN HIS VINE-COVERED 1920s ITALIANATE home, **Richard Shapiro** demonstrates his signature: the marriage of fine antiques and contemporary art.

A retired businessman, he opened Richard Shapiro Antiques and Works of Art in Los Angeles in 2002 to turn his avocation into a more full-time affair. It was a natural progression, as he had already spent more than three decades studying and collecting post-war contemporary art and period furniture. In the last ten years he has placed many of his acquisitions in his personal environment. It was here that he first put his ideas for fusing past and present to the test.

The result is at once refined and edgy, but with absolutely no trace of trendiness. Shapiro's expression through design seems an unselfconscious, completely devotional symphony using all the instruments that a conductor of interiors today has at his disposal. This conductor is in love with Roman antiquities, African sculpture, museum-quality period furniture, seventeenth and eighteenth-century Italian and French art, and twentieth-century conceptual art. He also loves Modern furniture, and Shapiro's new custom line Studiolo is influenced by notable twentieth-century French designers Jean-Michel Frank, Paul Dupré-Lafon, André Arbus, and Gilbert Poillerat, as well as the great twentieth-century Italian designer Renzo Mongiardino.

He adores them all. He is an individual who does not want to display a television or even telephone in the midst of one of his rooms' assemblages of his individually honed aesthetics. Yet he feels quite comfortable placing a seventeenth-century painting of St. Peter from Genoa on one side of an eighteenth-century Roman fireplace and Tadao Miyajima's circular L.E.D. wall piece on the other. He finds it enlivening to oppose a Joseph Hoffman chair with a primitive Welsh one. All these juxtapositions of art and furniture truly represent him, his tastes, what he feels is right.

One of the reasons he is smitten by these contemporary works is precisely because they keep all his centuries-old acquisitions from feeling too heavy and serious, as they might if kept sequestered by themselves. But as for contemporary appliances—adieu!

LOS ANGELES, CALIFORNIA

PHOTOGRAPHY BY DOUG MYERS

TOP: The dining room was added ten years ago and was designed by Richard Shapiro to combine feasting for both body and soul. From left: Robert Morris felt wall sculpture, 1978; Sol Lewitt "Open Cube"; Tadao Miyajima circular L.E.D. wall piece; eighteenth-century Roman fireplace; seventeenth-century painting of St. Peter from Genoa; Allan McCollum's 192-piece "The Surrogates"; French dining table, circa 1800; and nineteenth-century Regence-style chairs, slipcovered in muslin.

LEFT: Old master drawings set the inspirational flow in the library, gathering around a Louis XVI stone

fireplace and Louis XVI mirror. The stone and steel chow tables are from Studiolo by Richard Shapiro.

OPPOSITE PAGE: Above the living room's eighteenth-century stone fireplace, Richard Shapiro has chosen to place the literally off-the-wall selection of art - a stainless steel "implosion" sculpture by Ewerdt Hilgemann. The contrast between two periods, he says, makes us better appreciate each one. Then once again, he places a twentieth-century Joseph Hoffman chair opposite a primitive Welsh chair. The rug is by Stark. The low table in lacquer is one of Richard Shapiro's designs, Richard Shapiro Studiolo.

OPPOSITE PAGE: Originally an outdoor space that was later enclosed with glass, the gallery provides a sensual light-and-garden experience with, from left: a Joel Shapiro wood sculpture, 1986; a 1963 Gunter Uecker nail piece above a sixteenth-century French bench; a large geometric bronze by Tony Smith; and, in the foreground, the "Natura" bronze by Lucio Fontana, 1960.

TOP: The master bedroom has been totally rebuilt and designed by Richard Shapiro. The suede sofa and low lacquered table are by Studiolo through Richard Shapiro. At left, "Blind Time Drawing" by Robert Morris is situated above an eighteenth-century Italian console. The far corner holds an Austrian Biedermeier secretary. Shapiro designed the bed using eighteenth-century Indian textiles that he acquired in Jaipur.

RIGHT: Shapiro completely redesigned the master bathroom, covering all walls with a combination of mahogany, Fior di Pesca marble, and mirror. The marbles on the floor are Fior di Pesca, Negro Maquina, and Carrara. The head on the counter is Roman, fourth century.

QUEST FOR SERENITY

TOP: An ironwood walkway with a granite edge that holds in black river rock extends along the back of the house. RIGHT: The cedar entry hall doors, restored with the original stain color, combine frosted glass with clear to soften the bright afternoon sunlight, which falls on the home's southern side. The rug is an antique kilim. The planter is Japanese.

HAVING BEEN A STUDENT OF ZEN SINCE 1970, **CECILE BRADBURY** HAS long been drawn to the idea of a personal environment that expresses the simplicity and grace she finds in Zen instruction. When she found this house, built in 1961 as one of three for a family compound that expressed the same sentiment through great bones and many Japanese touches, she knew she was home.

Its only drawback was its small size, a matter she addressed by removing the former living and dining rooms and adjacent patio to create one large living space such as one finds in traditional Japanese houses. Opening up from the much lower entry, the 25-foot by 20-foot area with a 16-foot-high ceiling lends contrast, surprise, and a feeling of unending serenity.

Many of the home's existing attributes were left unchanged: the cedar-and-glass front doors, the original lighting fixtures, the Japanese sliding screens, the kitchen's alternating pink and clear skylights, and ash veneer cabinetry with Formica counters. For the new great room, she used much of the same design and materials palette that had existed before, so that all that is new does not appear to have been added on. The original floors, which were stained cement, have been replaced with bamboo throughout except for the guest bedroom where Bradbury placed a wool sisal carpet with a wooden border.

For furnishings, Bradbury combined her antique Asian treasures from her previous residence with other new ones—some made by the fine artisans and manufacturers she represents through The Bradbury Collection at the Pacific Design Center, Los Angeles.

For the garden, she worked with Keegan, a Zen monk and landscaper, building an ironwood walkway all around the back of the house and searching for boulders at Mount Baldy, handpicking each one for inspiration. As in every aspect of this home, the idea is that the majesty of the whole can only be as important as the reverence for each and every detail.

SOUTH PASADENA, CALIFORNIA

PHOTOGRAPHY BY ALEXANDER VERTIKOFF

Jacobsen. Dominating the far wall are a step tansu and a black lacquer Chinese double tansu, which is used as a media cabinet. The seating area at right features a black granite coffee table and a black chinoiserie table designed by the late Kalef Alaton. The two indigo wool area carpets were designed by Joan Weisman and made in Tibet.

TOP LEFT: The kitchen looking toward the living area: Bradbury retained the home's original ash veneer cabinets and Formica counters, as well as three-panel sliding bamboo doors. She also kept the original glass globe lighting fixtures, the pink, and natural skylights, finding them interesting reflections of the 1960s, and very Japanese in their shape and scale.

TOP: The guest room shows Bradbury's addition of antique sliding bamboo doors from Charles Jacobsen. The floor covering is wool sisal with cedar wood border. The sudari screens have decorative silk tassels, roll upwards, and can be hooked to ornamental brass hooks [not visible]. The chair, by Los Angeles designer Alwy Visschedyk, is eucalyptus wood. Bradbury found its companion inlaid table in Africa.

LEFT: The completely rebuilt and enlarged living area has a cathedral ceiling with solid beams from Oregon and custom wood windows and doors that slide open to the garden beyond. The low dining table at left is actually a Chinese bed that, with a futon, can be used for overnight guests. It is surrounded by upholstered stools with wooden borders that are more comfortable for most people than traditional Japanese dining cushions. The two stools by the window are by Scandinavian designer Hans Sandgren

TOAST TO ART DECO

TOP: Tartaglia designed the dining table with an elliptical glass top over a stainless steel base that has two levels, the lower one framed with maple and used as a service area. His custom-designed walnut and maple cabinet has a green marble top and contains porcelain and stemware. The Art Nouveau chandelier is French. The custom draperies are a deep red striped velvet and hang from large aluminum rings on a chrome bar.

RIGHT: The entrance has two existing arches of different sizes, classical features that the contemporary architect usually does not like. So he decided to play with them. To make them look equivalent in size, he made the larger arch, which opens onto the living/dining area, appear smaller by inserting an iron frame painted a copper color. He framed the smaller arch, which opens toward the kitchen and bedroom areas, with the same motif painted on the wall.

ANGELO VARDARO DESIGNS, REMODELS, AND RESTORES FURS, AND during the 1980s was at his height of celebrity and living in an expansive villa. However, when the effect of the ecologists' movement was to downsize his business, he decided to reduce his living space as well.

Asking architect **Angelo Luigi Tartaglia** to design his new home without knocking down any walls, he said what he mainly desired was a look of his favorite style, Art Deco, and a feeling reflecting the magnanimous spirit of his native Naples. Thus the only major revamping was the rewiring. Other than that, save for the décor, the original situation was left untouched even though the thoroughly contemporary architect had to deal with the structure's traditional character. Considering how completely fresh and up-to-the-minute is the final result, the achievement is remarkable.

The reason is that it is far easier for a designer to create an integrated environment—one that perfectly reflects the client's lifestyle and aspirations—when starting from scratch or when permitted to knock down walls. However, when the designer cannot make any changes to the pre-existing foundation, making adjustments that are completely in harmony with the original and, indeed, part of the same idea, can be a daunting process. This was doubly so for Tartaglia, since his client hoped to maintain the same fine quality of his previous home—not wanting to renounce his high style of living even while simplifying his environment and on a budget. In this case, the answer was not only possible but also fully achieved.

Vardaro lives by himself yet he loves to socialize and entertains at home frequently. Abetted by the warm feeling of his new surroundings along with his own hospitable personality, friends and family have found this home as perfect a gathering place as his former one, perhaps an even cozier and more welcoming one. The kitchen, newly furnished with Tartaglia's highly functional custom designs, still enables Vardaro to pursue his passion for cooking, while the audio/visual system throughout satisfies his love of music.

Along with Tartaglia's placement of his client's treasured collections and favorite fashion and cooking books amid much color and several stunning decorative wall treatments, Vardaro continues to feel that his southern Italian heart and soul are in their right place.

ROME, ITALY

PHOTOGRAPHY BY CRISTINA FIORENTINI

LEFT: The sitting and dining areas are defined by coconut-fiber rugs that are framed with brown. Horizontal shelves of rosewood provide ample room for collectibles and benefit from the warm glow of the Venetian glass light from Leucos.

TOP: The Art Deco desk from France and its 1940s chair are juxtaposed with a colorful floor lamp from Fontana Arte, reproduced from the Italian manufacturer's early twentieth-century archives. Tartaglia designed the maple and rosewood wall cabinet (one of a pair in this room) to represent the conclusion of his butterfly-wing wooden shelves. The collection is of crystal and glass from the 1920s to 1950s and includes Lalique, Daum and Baccarat.

OPPOSITE PAGE: The light fixture from Vardaro's old fashion design laboratory has been incorporated into the kitchen to complement the architect's functional design for the table, fabricated of steel and painted the color of aluminum. Its corners are of maple wood and top of glass. The folding chairs are from the 1970s and were previously located in the client's laboratory.

TOP: The unadorned queen-size bed plays up the interest of the Art Deco console and colorful watercolors and graphics, including a work by the Metaphysical artist Giorgio de Chirico (1888-1978).

RIGHT: To make the existing bathroom more inviting without structural changes, the architect applied wood paneling to all the walls and had them painted with an Art Deco motif. The floor is linoleum from Liuni Company.

FAR RIGHT: To enhance the existing wardrobe, the architect asked an artist to paint a rhythmic ribbon-like design on every door.

RENAISSANCE SENSIBILITY FOR A CLASSIC GENTLEMAN

TOP: Looking over the living room's porcupine-quill coffee table with its sand-cast candelsticks is the fireplace and Jean Dubuffet painting. A lavender-gray wall surface offers a softer version of the purple used elsewhere in this room. The fireplace face is detailed with walnut and has a marble threshold.

RIGHT: The living room's remodeled Saporiti sofa covered in a cotton velvet faces two forest green suede chairs, which are also early Saporiti pieces. The existing wall-to-wall carpet with a decorative border was left in place as it suited the refurbished space. The purple rose mirror glass cabinet at the far side of the room aesthetically divides the living room from the dining room and holds Chinese platters and small vases, many of sand-cast glass and all brought home by Kaufman during his travels. A collectible coffee table detailed with porcupine quills provides the necessary surface for appetizers and drinks.

JAMES KAUFMAN, HEAD OF A LARGE ACCOUNTING FIRM, LOVES classical music and reads extensively. In fact, he has read every volume on his library's teeming shelves. He involves himself in a host of outdoor activities. A sailboat and powerboat are anchored in the lagoon at the base of his property, which is surrounded by 30-foot-tall bamboo, a palm garden and magnificent royal palms overlooking Biscayne Bay and Key Biscayne.

Dealing with existing architectural constraints and many existing furnishings, **Dennis Jenkins and Associates** refurbished the home to make it more reflective of Kaufman's affinity for elegant entertaining and lush natural surroundings. New wall treatments were created for both interior and exterior, and many new elements were integrated with the old, including the addition of flooring, custom cabinetry, and one-off freestanding pieces. One of these custom one-off designs created by Jenkins specifically for this house is the dining room's mirrored breakfront, a hand-carved solid Cuban mahogany gem. In the library, to complement the fine detailing of its existing nineteenth-century-style design, Jenkins removed the heavy drapery and installed wide blade walnut shutters, new upholstery, and furnishings.

Here in South Florida where the light is unusually clear, the correct choice of color can be particularly challenging. While Jenkins has used this important design element to permit each room and exterior space to stand on its own—choosing Renaissance-inspired hues appropriate to his client's classic tastes—he took special care in making sure they would harmonize with the others in context of the architecture and the abundance and quality of light. The home is sited east-west and the morning sun is penetrating. The effect on color is particularly true with the natural lighting in the breezeway allowing the passage of sunlight to move through the home from sunrise to sunset.

It is interesting to note that this home—with unusual allusions to a neoclassical past via its idiosyncratic architectural and interior effects—is situated in Coconut Grove, which is eccentric, always liberal and non-conforming. The new design is as appropriate to its location as it is for James Kaufman himself.

MIAMI, FLORIDA

PHOTOGRAPHY BY LANNY PROVO

TOP AND LEFT: The dining room is scaled in proportion to its Sheraton table and Hepplewhite chairs, all in mahogany, and the fine handcrafted breakfront made of solid mahogany (only the inlaid marquetry is a veneer) and its felt-lined silver drawers and large cabinet space provide more than adequate storage for the owner's fine service. All are set against a background of soft lavender gray and off-white silk drapery and gray marble floor.

OPPOSITE PAGE: The library looks toward the entry foyer with the living room and dining room beyond. The English wingchair has been upholstered in a striped silk fabric and is situated with a reproduction of an English hand-embossed leather-topped desk. The carpet is forest-green velvet-finished broadloom. The library's wood detailing is English and based on libraries in the 1800s. In the entry, the Chinese scroll is framed in teakwood with a rosewood bench beneath.

TOP LEFT AND RIGHT: The breezeway offers a remarkably inviting gathering space, as it affords protection from the weather as well as a view over Key Biscayne, or just a wonderful meditative space. Pigskin suede Italian chairs, which are hand-carved, combined with an unusual coffee table base with an etched glass top, contrast with the rattan sofa and indoor/outdoor feeling, which is at once formal and informal in nature. The painted wood column holds a sand-cast Murano glass vase. Another table located nearby for occasional dining in the breezeway is honey onyx.

LEFT: The library's music stand always holds a dictionary at the ready. The shutters are fitted with 2.5-inch-wide mahogany blades and when weather permits, the windows are opened wide and the shutters allow breezes to gently come within. Dennis Jenkins based his design on the shutter design for both the library and the master bedroom after early Cuban shutters.

TOP: The master suite's bed is custom-framed with mahogany and welcomes with a silk bedspread and pillows, candle, and hurricane lamp. Nightstand and bedframe work as a built-in unit. The cabinet at left holds books and collections. Flooring is teak. A soothing French painting hovers above the Louis XVI dresser beyond. A Louis XVI cabinet houses this audiophile's collection of classical music.

TOP RIGHT: View through the pergola at the pool toward the guest room: the harlequin pattern of the wall and its Renaissance tones continue the interior's idiosyncratic surfaces to the exterior.

RIGHT: The view from the patio and breezeway offers a sweeping vista of sub-tropical Biscayne Bay. Beyond the patio is a lawn stretching 150 feet to the lagoon boat harbor. The chaise lounges are contemporary in nature while the surrounding patio and breezeway are eclectic.

BLENDING EAST AND WEST

TOP: The home is set within the Siskiyou Mountains overlooking Rogue Valley and with the 9,000-foot peak of Mt. McLoughlin in the distance.

RIGHT: Bold yellow exterior plaster is contrasted with blue/purple window frames. Signaling the Parrishes' international interests are large hand carved Nepali columns at the master bedroom balcony.

NESTLED IN THE SISKIYOU MOUNTAINS OVERLOOKING ROGUE VALLEY with views of pastoral farmland, the city of Medford, and the peak of Mt. McLoughlin, the home of Earl and Rosemary Parrish symbolizes the hope and beauty they extend to those near and far.

The project, designed by architect **Michael Helm** with **Bruce Richey**, architect of record, with lighting designer **Julia Rezek**, was based on the idea that a contemporary Mediterranean home was built on an ancient Roman ruin. The brick wall with arches (the ancient ruin) runs in and along the entire length of the house, hidden in some areas and exposed in others, with contemporary windows and modern plaster walls providing the structural skin of the Villa. The home's main raison d'être, however, lies in its expression of this couple's involvement with healing.

The Parrishes travel annually to Tibet and Nepal to provide plastic surgery to children who desperately need corrective procedures (Dr. Parrish is founder of Parrish Cosmetic & Plastic Surgery Center, and Mrs. Parrish, not a professional designer, but obviously knowledgeable, created the interiors for that office, which she oversees, as well as for their home). Many treasures they have collected on these trips have been used to adorn their home, including four large hand-carved Nepali columns now placed at the master bedroom exterior balcony, an exquisite collection of religious icon paintings, some of which are painted by Rosemary Parrish herself, and Tibetan altars that Julia Rezek turned into wall sconces.

The couple's comfort with color—from the bold yellow exterior plaster contrasted with blue/purple window frames to the joyful placement of their art's rainbow of hues—seems an extension of their gracious, hospitable, international personalities. So, too, does their understanding of the importance of light—using Rezek's expertise throughout to bring a warm illuminating definition to architecture and furnishings.

For two people involved with healing people in need throughout the world, and who continually welcome others interested in the same multi-cultural and philanthropic dimensions, their home is an ideal and fascinating blend of Eastern and Western influences.

CENTRAL POINT, OREGON

PHOTOGRAPHY BY KIM BUDD, SOL VISUAL DEVELOPMENT

OPPOSITE PAGE: The hallway joins the main entry to the master bedroom wing. The ceiling consists of a series of groin vaults, with a recessed cavity at the spring point of each vault, where linear uplighting is used to delineate the beauty of these ancient forms. Decorative wall sconces provide a soft ambient flow, and the exterior patio features a stone statue of St. Francis. His and her personal offices, the master suite, master bath, and a gymnasium are included in this master wing of the house.

TOP: The living room's comfortable seating area in front of the fireplace is surrounded by the Parrishes' international influences: Italian arches setting the backdrop for numerous Asian artifacts and Rosemary Parrish's collection of religious icon paintings, some of which she painted herself. This room is only a section of a larger living space, divided by the fireplace wall, and including another sitting area, the dining room, and a large granite top island, adjacent to the kitchen. Recessed accent lighting highlights artwork and architectural elements, while the large linear cove provides a soft romantic uplight.

RIGHT: The dining room has magnificent views out of three grand archway windows. Lighting designer Julia Rezek turned the Parrishes' two Tibetan altars, old portable folding altars used by monks while traveling, into wall sconces by rigidifying them, mounting them to the walls, and lining the inside surfaces with translucent rice paper to diffuse the light. Wall-mounted lights behind the altars silhouette the hand-carved designs and accent the ceramic plates below. Recessed accent lighting from above also brings out the texture and color of the hand-painted woodcarvings.

TOP: The kitchen has three floating granite islands for food preparation, for the cook-top, and for serving. This spacious arrangement is ideal for entertaining and allows for several people to work in the kitchen simultaneously. Behind the stained glass doorway is an ample pantry. A large skylight provides plenty of daylight, while recessed accent lighting illuminates task areas. The custom built-in wood cabinet contains all servingware and displays special stemware and dishware with integral lighting.

RIGHT AND OPPOSITE PAGE: The master bathroom provides each person with a sink area and a separate vanity area. Custom designed mirror frames are located above each sink, and a sumptuous raised bath tub is the focal point of the room. Dark wood floors and dark granite materials convey a rich, elegant feeling.

TRANQUILITY IN A TREE HOUSE

TOP AND RIGHT: The natural cedar decking and plank floor are hand-rubbed with a dull varnish. Door frames have been stained a dark bark color so that the screens seemingly disappear. Glass is clear, deliberately not tinted as the forest offers ample screening from sun.

THE MAJESTY IS IN ITS SIMPLICITY. THE SECOND HOME OF TWO MEN— one a brilliant litigator, the other involved in financial services—it allows them to get away from their urban Mies Van der Rohe Chicago apartment (renovated by the same firm that designed this second home) and have peace and tranquility, practicality and comfort, in the country on the river. Both boat people, avid about good taste, living close to the land keeps them humble.

They already had a home here beside the river, but it did not allow for their large multi-generational family gatherings of forty to fifty to be at ease and have one great room. Now, through the creativity of **Powell/Kleinschmidt**'s **Thomas L. Boeman**, **Robert D. Kleinshmidt,** and **Donald D. Powell**, they do.

It is just a short walk from the existing main house through a glass-enclosed link. An all-cedar rectangular room with French doors and porches on three sides, it is a pyramid soaring amid the trees. It was Powell's vision to put the addition on cylindrical columns and, rather than walk up and down stairs, cross directly over from the first house, which is built at a higher elevation. Just a few steps from the first house they feel miles away—soaring 27 feet higher than the low land and just 60 feet from the river.

Pouring the circular concrete columns without disturbing any existing trees was a triumph. Leaving the spiral tracery on the concrete columns of the removed sona tubes, part of the charm of the method and its economy, was a further aesthetic accomplishment.

French doors all around establish the rhythm and sense of a Mid-Western porch and, with screens and ceiling fan, enable cross breezes to serve as au-natural air conditioning most of the time during warm weather and further establish the unpretentious feeling. Forced-air heating and the fireplace (not shown) keep body and soul nourished during winter.

The home conveys the sense of being at ease—from the welcoming largess of the firemen's chairs to the simple sturdy upholstery, from the rug's traditional Native American pattern to the rugged wood heirlooms.

The one and only thing that is precious here is the comforting, hospitable, and natural environment.

SAUGATUCK, MICHIGAN

PHOTOGRAPHY BY CHRISTOPHER BARRETT, HEDRICH-BLESSING

OPPOSITE PAGE: A kilim rug woven in an early Native American design provides the foundation for the rest—firemen's chairs stained the color of Dijon mustard, an amply sized 100-year-old pine table used for large family dinners and table games, an old family heirloom chest used for the coffee table. The sofa's masculine leather upholstery is juxtaposed with the seat and back cushions in softer transportation gros point cloth. Two pairs of wicker chairs have been painted a brown brick red to relate to the rug.

RIGHT: Large, appropriately no-nonsense fans, combined with the open French doors, enable air conditioning to be natural save for the hottest weather. Ample indirect lighting and uplighting brings out the warmth of the wood and lines of the ceiling with its exposed metal tie rods. Any form of window treatment was deemed unnecessary, transparency everything —even at night when a year's worth of trial and error has resulted in the same vision of an illuminated forest seen during the day.

WHERE NATURE GOES POP

TOP: As do its owners, the 9,000-square-foot, two-story house relates to the landscape, both in the rich materiality of the exterior brickwork and in the spanning, horizontal gesture of the roof lines. Both timeless and practical, it allows them to seamlessly incorporate their contemporary art collection amid their natural refuge.
RIGHT: A Morris Louis painting sends a vibrant crescendo over the living room's quieter notes of the reissue Le Corbusier chairs, vintage Dunbar 1960s sofa, and early twentieth-century Biedermeier tables and chairs. The expansive living/dining area provides flexibility for entertaining both large and intimate gatherings.

IT SEEMED LIKE A WEDDING IN SHAKESPEARE'S "A MIDSUMMER Night's Dream." A collection of Pop and Modern art in an earthly sylvan setting looked impossible, but come morning, this marriage still rings true.

In a home influenced by both Japanese and Craftsman traditions as well as its region's noted "Prairie style" of architecture, works by such artists as Andy Warhol, David Hockney, Fernand Leger, Joseph Albers, and Joan Miró feel at home. It is a compliment to the owners' inventive flair for dramatic juxtapositions.

A retired theater owner and his wife appreciated the inspiring, unaffected beauty of their two-and-one-half-acre site overlooking two lakes and its proximity to numerous early twentieth-century architectural treasures (by Eliel and Eero Saarinen and Frank Lloyd Wright). They asked **McIntosh Poris Associates** to build a 9,000-square-foot, two-story house, inviting the firm to pair nature with things wrought by man.

The design was intentionally kept subdued, always emphasizing the strength of the landscape. Outside, the home's rich brickwork and spanning, horizontal roof lines are totally devoted to their relationship to the hill in which they are ensconced. Inside, the furniture, primarily a modern/antique mix, is meshed with a few pieces and built-ins designed by McIntosh Poris to provide subtle transitions between architectural shell and living spaces. Special detailing includes door and cabinet hardware designed by metal students at nearby Cranbrook Academy of Art; double-paned windows with no corner mullions, but connected with clear glass glue; carpeting of visible undersides of stair treads; and antique fabrics made into pillows.

Apparent throughout is the owners' predilection for providing a home for mementoes collected from around the world and a second home for guests/family.

The architecture team includes **Michael Poris**, AIA, principal in charge; **Doug McIntosh**, principal; and **Christine Kennedy, Mark Carrabio, Bradley Maddalena, Russell Baltimore, Patricia Boyle, Donna Varonovich,** and **Derk Wolkotten**. Interiors are by **Gayle Camden, GSC Design**. Landscape is by **Ken Weikal Landscape Architects** with **Debra Silver/ Detroit Garden Works**.

BLOOMFIELD HILLS, MICHIGAN

PHOTOGRAPHY BY BALTHAZAR KORAB

LEFT: Extremely rare Roy Lichtenstein wallpaper, which was installed in the owners' previous house, is framed as art in the "Mod sitting room" with original acrylic and leather furniture from the 1970s.

TOP: The living room's baby grand piano is situated near the central hall and dining area for multi-purpose use while entertaining. Brick interior elements are sheathed with mahogany. Punctuating the hall and visible from dining, living, and hall areas are artworks by Andy Warhol and David Hockney.

OPPOSITE PAGE: The sitting room's Montis chairs and ottomans are underscored by a nineteenth-century Oushak rug, while the high note above the fireplace is a painting by Fernand Leger. Interior elements, such as columns, walls, baseboards, doors, and windows, are delineated in mahogany wood.

LEFT: In the dining room, an early twentieth-century cabinet from India next to a painting by Joan Miró provides a surprising juxtaposition.

TOP: In the library, a highly urbane grouping of Joseph Albers paintings, Georgetti chairs, and a 1970s A.I. (Atelier International) sofa provide counterpoint to the landscaped tranquility beyond.

RIGHT: The expansive kitchen features stainless steel and verde marble with custom-made rice-paper-backed window cabinets. Piercing the serenity is a Sue Marx painting.

STAGE SET FOR DAILY LIFE

TOP: The home's colored stucco and wooden deck stand out amid its lush hillside setting. Punched-out windows checker its exterior, providing ample natural light inside.
PHOTOGRAPHY BY ALEKS ISTANBULLU
RIGHT: The living room's spacious walls provide ample room for displaying Gabor Csupo and Bret Crain's eclectic art collection, including prints by Matisse and Picasso. Furnishings include a custom-made sectional Italian sofa and an Eero Aarnio "Ball Chair."
PHOTOGRAPHY BY ERIC LAIGNEL

THE PERFECT SOLUTION FOR THE FAMILY OF A PERFORMANCE artist and entertainment executive involved in children's animation? A real-life stage set!

Gabor Csupo and his wife Bret Crain asked **Aleks Istanbullu Architects** to replace a neglected 1950s house with one much more suited to their needs for children's bedrooms, master suite, large interior spaces for frequent entertaining, and screening room with ample media storage. The resulting 7,500-square-foot, three-story home combines a sequence of spaces that not only fulfills those requirements, but also feels as lively as Gabor's signature television show, "Rugrats."

The house feels so animated that it is called Hinge House—you can't miss its Lego-like assemblage of parts in the visually obvious connections between three distinct components. The first is a two-story volume that includes children's rooms, family room, utility room, home offices, screening room, and media archives. The second component is a sculpted third-floor master suite that sits tree-house-like amid the steep hillside's foliage. The third component, a steel-framed two-story volume below the master suite, is an indoor-outdoor space where a dining platform, family room balcony, and stairway wrapped around an interior stone koi pond evoke a joyful sense of theater.

Exposed steel beams and roofing respond to Gabor and Bret's request for an industrial-techno look and lend further to the improvisational feel. Interior treatments, surfaces, and volumes continue the feeling of dramatic fun. Furniture is a mix of both whimsical and serious pieces, ranging from streamlined Italian to handmade glass, and art ranges from Matisse and Picasso prints to vintage Hungarian movie posters and, of course, "Rugrats" art. Every detail of the hybrid assortment expresses Bret and Gabor's belief that life should be approached *playfully*.

The design team included **Aleks Istanbullu**, AIA, principal, his firm's project manager **Tom Nohr** and team member **Arminda Diaz**, as well as lighting design firm **Tim Thomas & Associates** and **Paul Lewis Landscape Architecture**.

LOS ANGELES, CALIFORNIA

OPPOSITE PAGE: A stairway wraps around the koi pond, connecting the living room with the dining platform. Colorful sculptures with an aquatic theme, including a 15-foot submarine, are suspended above the living room's koi pond. A long, glass window offers a view of the underwater world.
PHOTOGRAPHY BY WELDON BREWSTER

RIGHT: The colorful, light-filled dining room is a theatrical yet domestic space. Its snaking chandelier lowers the height of the ceiling and playfully echoes the circular holes of the dining chairs.
PHOTOGRAPHY BY GREY CRAWFORD

TOP: Exposed steel beams and a painted corrugated metal ceiling create a techno-industrial feeling. Color is used to break down the expansive spaces into playful pieces, such as the dark, Venetian-plastered koi pond and the bright red playroom balcony overlooking the living room.

PHOTOGRAPHY BY WELDON BREWSTER

RIGHT: Stainless steel kitchen cabinetry imparts an industrial look, while a comical collection of sculptures appeals to a lighter sensibility.

PHOTOGRAPHY BY WELDON BREWSTER

TOP: Situated on the third floor, the master bath looks out to the redwood terrace, hillside, and San Fernando Valley. Skylights over the tub, painted white to provide a pattern within the blue ceiling, admit natural light by day.
PHOTOGRAPHY BY GREY CRAWFORD

RIGHT: The original clover-leaf pool, designed by Paddock Pools in the 1950s, has been refinished and updated. Legend has it that Esther Williams was filmed swimming here.
PHOTOGRAPHY BY WELDON BREWSTER

YEN FOR QUIET AND ORDER

TOP AND RIGHT: To replace the storage space lost with the removal of built-in shelving flanking the existing limestone fireplace, the designers added freestanding units and a custom made storage cabinet covered in duck egg blue leather to conceal audio equipment. The leather armchair is generously proportioned, but low enough to work well with the sofa, both of which are by French furniture designer Phillipe Hurel. As this house does not have a deep front garden, the designers chose sheer Roman blinds with a solid blind on top to provide privacy. The client's ceramics collection includes these by Italian designer Marina Rinaldi.

EVEN WHEN WE SIMPLIFY OUR HOME ENVIRONMENTS, WE SHOULD no more completely discard our lifelong aesthetic characteristics than we should our family name. They are part of us, our comfort, and our identity. Yes, we might be tired of the rigorous turmoil of our former domicile. Surely the clutter could well be left behind, as well as too great a material responsibility, but not the feeling. Please keep the feeling. This homeowner did.

A successful businessman who has a heavy work-related traveling schedule, this client of **Carden Cunietti** wanted a simple, pared-down serenity most of all when he returns to his home in London. Especially since he does not often entertain, but prefers instead to read or play sports, his main need was for a personal refuge created just for him.

This search for quietude was reflected in his preference for a subdued color palette of pale neutrals with lilac, duck egg blue, and sage green as accents, and for a touch of traditional furnishings without feeling encumbered by too many of them.

Every stroke taken by **Audrey Carden** and **Eleanora Cunietti** has brushed the rooms with an airy lightness. They removed existing red wallpaper, replaced built-ins that gave a closed-in feeling with less cumbersome, free-standing pieces, and contrasted the pieces of dark wood furniture with others of acrylic and glass. Window treatments and the stairway carpet runner are cream colored to provide uplift yet are bordered with chocolate velvet or dark leather to work with the wood. The dining room carpet was replaced with parquet wood flooring laid in a traditional herringbone pattern and running from the hallway through the dining room to the garden to unify the space with one spare, clean sweep.

As the client did not entertain extensively, he wished for the dining room to double as a morning room—hence the additional furnishings there include daybed and comfortable armchair for reading.

Equally expressive of the client's needs and his insistence on order was his desire for an organized approach to handling his wardrobe. The designers persuading him to dedicate one bedroom solely for use as a dressing room proved to be the ideal solution as well as the crowning glory of one man's quest for a peaceful getaway in the city.

DULWICH, ENGLAND

PHOTOGRAPHY BY ROBERT GREGORY

TOP, LEFT AND FAR LEFT: The dining room doubles as a morning room with the addition of daybed and table by American designer Chris Lehrecke, suede armchair, and parchment-covered side table. The large-scale buffet by Modenature is ideal for storage. Above the daybed, a Joan Miró print adds color and focus amid the home's continuing neutral palette, as does the modern Flos lighting fixture on the side table and glass lamp bases on the buffet.

TOP: In the master bedroom, when existing built-in wardrobes were removed to give a more spacious feel, the amount of storage space was not sacrificed as the client agreed to turn a second bedroom into one large closet/dressing room. Here the accent color amid the neutral scheme is lilac, with suede-like wall covering lending textural warmth. A Murano glass lamp with gray silk pleated shade and two lamps by Michel Taurel atop side tables by Christian Liagre add to the precisely selected collection. The Nan Golden photograph emphasizes the room's sense of calm.

RIGHT: In a former bedroom, an Italian dressing room system offers a flexible storage solution for all types of clothing. However, the way it looks and works in reality depends on the person using it. Fortunately this bachelor is very tidy! The room's other furnishings include a drawer unit, free-standing mirror framed with leather, a settee for sitting while putting on shoes, and two leather laundry baskets for separating white clothing from dark. Above the chest is an Andy Warhol print of Mohammed Ali.

COOL LOFT FOR DOC BLUE

TOP: The historic Kingman Building, a former pharmaceutical warehouse restored and renovated by Elliott + Associates Architects, is located above the Bricktown Canal. Doc Blue's loft is on the top floor and commands the three large windows at right.

RIGHT: Upon entering, people see fluorescent blue light glowing through a wall of glass block. Then they come around to the front hall, to the original warehouse floors—wide segments of pinewood—and realize this is not a normal experience. Once inside the entry vestibule, one is greeted with the image of Doc Blue in his Ray-Ban glasses, wearing a fedora, and playing a harmonica.

THE PROJECT WAS ALREADY ONE OF THE MOST INTERESTING IN THE career of **Rand Elliott**, **Elliott + Associates Architects:** it involved restoring the 1941 Kingman Building, a pharmaceutical warehouse on Bricktown Canal. He and his associate **Brian Fitzsimmons** were creating new spaces within this urban center redevelopment project and tourist attraction, including two restaurants below and two lofts above. People were taking rides on the canal boats and jogging along the new raised sidewalk to see what wonderful new thing was happening in their Oklahoma City. But "interesting" took on another meaning entirely when Elliott and Fitzsimmons met Doc Blue, owner of the loft on the the top floor.

By day, Dr. French Hickman is well-known in the community as an orthodontist. By night, he becomes Doc Blue, a blues singer and harmonica player. The club where he plays on Thursday through Saturday nights, The Biting Sow, is just 300 feet down the canal.

Elliott + Associates' assignment was to reflect the persona of this larger-than-life former stockcar racer, this important professional's nocturnal alter ego, in a 2,560-square-foot space that would be the ideal hangout for his blues pals and also to impress his lady friends. Inserting two levels plus a mezzanine in the loft's significant 16-foot height, Elliott added the kitchen where Doc can keep one of his welcoming gourmet recipes constantly bubbling (to Doc, cooking, music, and camaraderie are all one inseparable song). Among Elliott's other snuggery appointments are a snooker table, a metal corner fireplace, and an appropriately 1960s-style pit complete with typical 1960s bachelor-pad shag carpet. The carpet is blue, of course, as are the walls, lights, and cabinetry—all reiterating Doc Blue's night magic. The original brick walls and wood beams have been retained and left exposed. Those things that are new, such as the cable lighting and, of course, Doc Blue's own stainless steel cable handrail that reflects what he does by day to correct the position of clients' teeth, are clearly represented. Elliott did not want any new element to try to act old in this historic building. Doc's favorite furnishings from the past, including the childhood saddle that he used to ride atop Topsy, add further notes of warmth and surprise.

Judging from the constant gatherings here amid the most jovial spirits in the world of blues, the space works extremely well.

OKLAHOMA CITY, OKLAHOMA

PHOTOGRAPHY BY ROBERT SHIMER, HEDRICH-BLESSING

FIRST FLOOR PLAN

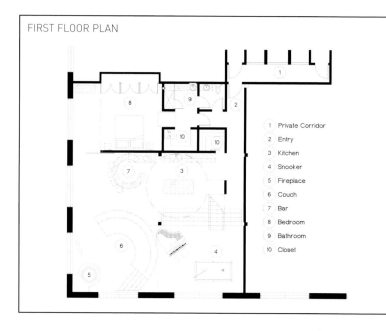

1. Private Corridor
2. Entry
3. Kitchen
4. Snooker
5. Fireplace
6. Couch
7. Bar
8. Bedroom
9. Bathroom
10. Closet

LEFT: Still on the first level, guests join around a corner fireplace at a beatstyle1960s pit, incorporating Doc Blue's former home's curved-wood-upholstered seating unit with shelving at back, now all painted blue and fitted with blue fabric cushions. The blue carpet is shag. The cable lighting presents an honest foray into currency without pretending to be part of the original building.

TOP: Doc Blue's kitchen of delights is appointed with a curved counter and bar-height stools (at left). Elliott + Associates added a horizontal beam to the original vertical column to support the newly created mezzanine. The stainless steel cable handrail, which Doc Blue wanted to weave himself (as he does this every day in miniature when practicing orthodontics), connects the stainless steel cable at the stair and mezzanine. At lower right is the snooker table and gathering area.

TOP: A favorite memory of Dr. French Hickman, "Doc Blue," is the saddle of his childhood horse Topsy, who would take him every morning to fetch the mail for his parents.

RIGHT: Behind the pit is the entrance to the downstairs bedroom—the master bedroom since Doc Blue stays up all night and likes to wander around to the kitchen and fireplace/pit amenities. The dark finished blinds knock out daylight and protect Doc Blue's nocturnal tendencies. The antique hutch is from Doc Blue's collection of family memorabilia.

INSPIRED BY LAND AND SEA

TOP: A sunset view of the house taken from the seaside reveals the architecture's abstract composition of concrete volumes and play of colors dominated by the vivid terra-cotta hue inspired by the site's natural soil.
RIGHT: The rooftop of the terrace next to the pool has been designed to give protection from the sun while enhancing the play of light. The floor of the pool is covered with ceramic, mostly black to give the effect of a deep lagoon. However, the stairs leading into the pool are of travertine marble, providing continuity from the terrace.

WHEN A YOUNG ENTREPRENEUR COUPLE MOVED TO ISRAEL, THEY found a site ideally suited to their passion for sports and the sea—139 square feet of dark red sandy land on top of a cliff north of Tel Aviv with spectacular views of the Mediterranean. To create a house that would adapt to the surroundings and the climate, they turned to the architectural firm of **Legorreta + Legorreta**.

The result reflects not only the dramatic setting, but the clients' lifestyle as well. Family gatherings revolve around a central courtyard that can be flooded and converted into a fountain, bringing a fresh interior environment in contrast to the rough dynamics of its surroundings. There is, however, no wish to shut out nature here, and the constant juxtaposition of the peaceful interior and the strong sweeps of wondrous earthiness beyond play a major part in the home's character. Indeed, the design includes a system to open the windows electrically so that, when weather permits, there is an abundant interaction between interior and exterior that is remarkably enlivening.

Shaped by walls, towers, and volumes painted different tones of oxide, the structure is intended to heighten the already commanding views by framing them. The view from the entrance carries forth to a towering russet arch framing the view to the patio. The living room's walls are like grand repetitive prosceniums opening to the glorious scene beyond.

The interior spaces themselves have each been given a distinctive identity—the family room's strong relationship to the pool, the dining room's cylindrical shape overlooking the cactus garden, the children's rooms each having its own special patio. The main bedroom, located on the second floor where there is also a small studio and rooftop space for sunbathing, is graced with a view seemingly extending to infinity.

Architecture by LEGORRETA + LEGORRETA: Ricardo Legorreta, Victor Legorreta, Noe Castro. Design team: Gerardo Alonso. Executive architect: Adolfo Levy.

SHFAYIM, ISRAEL

PHOTOGRAPHY BY YONA SCHLEY

LEFT: The living room with view to the pool and the sea: the flooring here and throughout the home's public areas is travertine marble washed with acid. Each piece of marble is cut by measure to fit with the line of the walls. The furniture is custom designed for the house by Legorreta + Legorreta. Spot lighting is hidden between the beams. Wall-mounted lighting fixtures are made of wood and finished with the walls' same texture coating.

TOP: The corridor leads toward the dining room, terrace, and swimming pool area. The wall on the right is marked by special detailing for light and concludes with a richly colored arch to emphasize the vaulted ceiling and the direction toward the sea.

TOP RIGHT AND RIGHT: A custom-designed massive wooden door provides a grand entry to the dining room. The table's shape was designed in response to the circular shape of the space, which is defined on the exterior by the color purple. A slice of that strong purple hue is brought into the room's interior, pierced by a small round window. A huge floor-to-ceiling curved window looks out toward the cactus garden, inspired by Israel's natural landscape and reflected in a mirror to bring continuity to the massive wall beyond.

TOP: A soft purple hue defines the interior courtyard that serves as the family gathering space or it can be flooded and converted into a fountain.
RIGHT: From the second floor's studio, access to the roof provides a view of the site's farthest horizon and the home's interplay of various shapes and volumes.

CONTEMPORARY FARMHOUSE

TOP: The front elevation with its contemporary interpretation of a French-Canadian barn expresses Landry's feeling for Quebec, Canada, where he was born. The rectangular home is approached on a one-mile-long entry road that passes through garage to car court at entry (second level of the home). The garage is designed as a crib barn. The house is constructed of concrete blocks and 100-year-old reclaimed barn wood from Quebec. RIGHT: The two-story rear elevation shows the pool at night, with the home's barn shape flanked by two satin-finished sheet metal silos, which house four bathrooms. The roof is capped with a clerestory window. Exposed trusses shade balconies and decks. A stream wraps around the 27-foot diameter pool inspired by a water tank. The pool's shell is a corrugated metal tank, the interior pressure sprayed with Gunite.

THE SIMPLE BEAUTY AND CULTURAL HERITAGE OF A PICTURESQUE French-Canadian farm have been transported to a dramatic eleven-acre hilltop site overlooking the Pacific Ocean. Noted residential architect **Richard Landry** has seamlessly infused elements of a 100-year-old farmhouse into a unique contemporary design to create a private residence—for himself!

In a departure from the Mediterranean, Tuscan, and European-themed estates he creates for his upscale client base, Landry's design for his own home innovatively references his childhood farm roots and the distinct architectural sensibility of his adopted Southern California lifestyle.

Believing that a home should be an expression of one's emotions and memories, a belief he has applied in his designs for others in Asia and the Caribbean as well the United States, Landry refers here to his native Quebec, Canada. Timber recovered from Quebec, the inspiration for the home's barn shape, is pitted with wormholes and bug marks and lacquered not by paint but by one hundred years of snowy and rainy weather. Landry continues the process—leaving the wood with no protection so it can continue forth in its aging process.

From a simple rectangular floor plan to an inventive use of texture and light to an eclectic selection of materials and furnishings, Landry's hand is in every detail and reflects his passion for his rural heritage. Original barn wood is used for structural and interior design elements; two aluminum-clad grain-silo-shaped forms at either end contain the bathrooms; corrugated metal is used to create a water tank-inspired pool; a large rolled steel boiler-like form becomes the fireplace in the great room.

The farm and rural references are completely integrated in the design, making the most of its southwestern location. Large sliding glass doors in the great room and kitchen welcome outdoor excursions to patios, pool, and breathtaking views. Clerestory windows pay further tribute to the area's clement weather. Contemporary amenities, such as an up-to-date professionally equipped kitchen, a state-of-the-art gym, and European-styled steam room complete with rain showers, offer an exceedingly civil range of comfortable living not possible a century ago.

MALIBU, CALIFORNIA

PHOTOGRAPHY BY ERHARD PFEIFFER

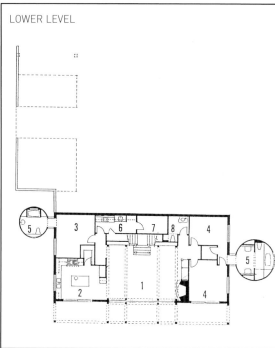

LOWER LEVEL

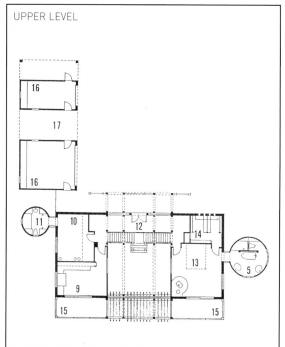

UPPER LEVEL

TOP: The barn in the distance is the first structure on Landry's property that one sees when driving up the one-mile road to the main house. A long, private driveway winds in front of the stables and crosses a bridge over a waterfall and koi pond.

OPPOSITE PAGE: The walls of the foyer, extending upward from the great room, are unfinished, untreated wood barn siding, as is the wood on all doors. The door handles have been retrieved from horse carriages. The exposed framing and rafters are of rough-cut timber. Other materials include straw-colored concrete block and, instead of paint, yellow beeswax as used in ancient Egypt has been applied to a layer of acrylic plaster to enhance the natural beauty of the walls. The 3/4-inch guardrails at the top of the stairs feature fields of cattails based on a drawing by Landry, referencing marshlands of Quebec.

TOP LEFT: View overlooking the great room from the master bedroom across to the similarly shuttered home office. The trellis below the clerestory window on the left abuts the glass, creating the illusion of transparency. At right is a split-faced concrete block wall, with all blocks made with two different colors to create the feeling of natural stone.

TOP RIGHT: In the master bathroom, the polished book-matched marble floor in calico-cat tones was imported from Greece. The ceiling beams are barn wood. The custom designed side tables are alder wood.

LEFT: Landry, who likes to socialize while cooking, designed his professionally equipped kitchen with an open floor plan and large center island to allow for easy maneuvering. Major appliances have a Viking blue finish, adding warmth to the highly functional space. At night, the room glows with the soft light from a candle-burning chandelier.

OPPOSITE PAGE: A cast iron pot-belly wood burning stove in the corner adds warmth to the master bedroom's country charm and is finished in the same Viking blue as the kitchen appointments. The floating ceiling conceals indirect lighting above the Swedish iron bed and antique Swedish bench. An area rug brings barefoot comfort to the polished pecan floor. An old Mexican door has been turned into a coffee table. The pastel drawing is by Colorado artist Ted Larsen.

EMBRACING THE LAND

TOP: An important part of the experience of the property is the mile-long journey in from Red Hawk Road. The road moves through thick stands of oaks, crossing Lone Man Creek, before rising up to the edge of the large meadow where the house is located. Finally, the road circumvents a cactus patch to arrive at the west side of the house with its covered arcade.

RIGHT: The main living/dining room centers on a larger masonry fireplace. The wooden ceiling adds to the warm and rustic feeling of the The West Texas Sandstone of a finer coursing. The Lasners also envisioned their house as a place for their growing collection of art, including "Good Evening" by Vadim Chazov over the mantel and sculptures by Charles Umlauf.

CARL AND HELEN LASNER SPENT MANY YEARS THINKING ABOUT WHERE to put a house on their 135-acre property in the Hill Country. Carl was drawn to a large meadow surrounded by hills, and edged with oaks and large stands of prickly pear cactus, an area where breezes rise up from the adjacent arroyo and wash across the grasses. When he stood at that site, he knew he was home. When **Overland Partners Architects** came on board, they confirmed it.

As Carl and Helen, previously from Austin, thought of living here on a permanent basis with their teenage children, they envisioned comfort, coziness, and light, as well as ample private areas for dining, reading, meditating, and bathing—in every case being connected to nature. In the context of this site, that meant creating a place nestled into the trees while capturing the long views in multiple directions and engaging the land.

The architects' answer was placing the home's 5,000 square feet in a long, galley-shaped plan, typically one room deep so that natural light and breezes inhabit every corner. Covered outdoor spaces further the feeling of physical and visual rootedness to the landscape, as do the materials palette of stone and wood—the latter especially appropriate as the Lasners own Austin Hardwoods, a large hardwood lumber distribution company. From the seemingly infinitude of pecan, cherry, and cypress for floors, ceilings, and cabinetry, to the limestone grotto dining area with its large stone fireplace making outdoor meals inviting even in winter, to (yes!) the foot-lighted stone stairway wrapping up and around a sandstone cistern with a hot tub at its destination: nature at the Lasner home is most definitely embraced.

Soon after the Lasners began living in the house, Carl mentioned that he and Helen used to travel far and wide to stay at beautiful, serene places connected to their indigenous cultures and landscapes. Now their favorite vacation spot is right where they live!

Overland Partners Architects: Robert L. Shemwell, Principal in Charge/Principal Architect; Steve Kline, Project Architect; Karin Shelton, Project Team.

WIMBERLEY, TEXAS

PHOTOGRAPHY BY PAUL BARDAGJY

FLOOR PLAN

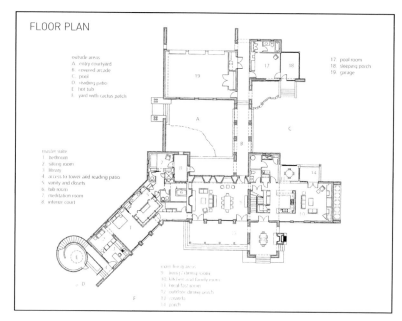

outside areas
A. entry courtyard
B. covered arcade
C. pool
D. reading patio
E. hot tub
F. yard with cactus patch

17. pool room
18. sleeping porch
19. garage

master suite
1. bedroom
2. sitting room
3. library
4. access to tower and reading patio
5. vanity and closets
6. tub room
7. meditation room
8. interior court

main living areas
9. living / dining room
10. kitchen and family room
11. breakfast room
12. outdoor dining porch
13. veranda
14. porch

TOP LEFT AND TOP RIGHT: One of the home's best spaces is the covered dining porch, designed for year-round use. Though it is open-air, a large fireplace makes it warm and inviting, celebrating the out-of-doors even during winter months.

ABOVE: The hot tub off the master bedroom wing is elevated in a cylindrical sandstone container that references the cistern at the Lady Bird Johnson Wildflower Center in Austin, Texas, also designed by Overland Partners.

RIGHT: Pecan is used extensively throughout the house, including the wood floors and kitchen cabinets. The wall separating the kitchen from the family room does not extend to ceiling, thus visually connecting the two areas, permitting the flow of light and air.

INDOOR/OUTDOOR

TOP: From the street, one senses a mysterious courtyard compound beyond. An exterior skeleton of steel ties the main house and guest house together and becomes a framework for the external sun shades. The orange and burnt-sienna-colored fabric shades can be automatically controlled up and down as well as across. Photography by Julius Shulman with Juergen Nogai.

RIGHT: Even when sun sails are withdrawn, the skeleton of steel enlivens the exterior with a sense of nautical rigging, appropriate to the locale near the Pacific Ocean. The balcony above the front door (far right) makes the entry experience intimate at a height of 7 feet-5 inches. Photography by Julius Shulman with Juergen Nogai.

ARCHITECT **STEVEN EHRLICH** AND HIS WIFE, AUTHOR AND MAGAZINE editor Nancy Griffin, planned their home as a flexible compound for family gatherings, overnight guests, and personal rejuvenation. It is no wonder that their home should have one space opening onto another and another, with a variety of multi-use areas. Augmented by its being built of raw, honest materials reflective of the bohemian grittiness of Venice, the home's dominant feeling is casual, down-to-earth ease.

A key requirement for Steven, founder of **Steven Ehrlich Architects**, was to maximize volume, light, and privacy on his narrow 43 x 132 foot urban corner lot while being sensitive to the scale and context of the area's twentieth-century traditional beach bungalows. At two stories plus a mezzanine level, the house, as well as its separate garage/guest room, is taller than most homes in the neighborhood. He was able to solve the problem of scale by setting his home back from the streets and shielding it from adjacent views with two existing large pine trees and a palm, each gracing one of three distinct courtyards. Walls and landscaping screen the two sides of his house that face the street corner.

The structure's wood-and-steel frame is outlined by a steel exoskeleton from which automatic light scrims roll down to shield the front façade from the western sun. The 15.5-foot-high living/dining area opens up on three sides—to the lap pool on the west with sliding glass doors, to the north courtyard and guest house with pocketing glass doors, and to the garden to the south through pivoting metal doors. All aspects fit the Ehrlichs' desire for their home to be environmentally sensitive and sustainable. When open entirely to the elements, the home is an airy pavilion, with temperate ocean breezes making air conditioning unnecessary. The concrete slab underneath the entire structure absorbs the sun's warmth in the winter and has a radiant heat source for cold nights. Photovoltaic sunshades store and augment energy.

Most importantly, the Ehrlichs are enjoying a home that truly lives up to their wish for flexibility, relaxation, and renewal.

VENICE, CALIFORNIA

PHOTOGRAPHY BY JULIUS SHULMAN WITH JUERGEN NOGAI

LEFT: Beyond the pool, a sliding glass door enables a free flow of space into the living areas. The chair in the foreground is by Frank Gehry. The couch and table are by David Albert Design. The diptych painting is by Ed Moses (2004). The wool carpet is from Nepal. The leather poufs are from Nigeria. Boomerang chairs (in walnut) are by Richard Neutra. Photography by Erhard Pfeiffer.

TOP: A view toward master bedroom patio shows steel exoskeleton with the energy efficient, sail-like shades down, adding color and billowing movement in response to the ocean breezes. Photography by Erhard Pfeiffer.

RIGHT: Oversized glass pivot doors with aluminum frames make one space of the living, dining, kitchen, and courtyard. The south courtyard between the main house and studio/guesthouse is the home's most prominent open space, features a radiant concrete patio and built-in seating bench. The kitchen is only 7.5 feet high, a transformation from the 15.5-foot main space that allows visitors to feel the importance of the primary living space. However, the kitchen plays an important part in the Erhlichs' lives, as Nancy loves to cook and has the knack for making the process a communal affair. The table in the foreground is zebrawood, with bench seating and leather pillows. In the kitchen, custom stainless tables/shelves are partnered with a center island of walnut cabinetry topped by Carrera marble. Photography by Julius Shulman with Juergen Nogai.

LEFT: The master bedroom's sliding glass door allows a full opening to the elastomeric decking and view to the guest house/studio. The roof soffit is solid Latvian birch plywood. The prints above the bed are by Paul Jacoulet. Traditional Japanese fir cabinets serve as bedside tables. The Parsons table of Latvian plywood is by Joel Bell and Paul Down. Photography by Erhard Pfeiffer.

TOP: At the mezzanine level, the steel and glass bridge is a high-tech counterpoint to the primal bead-blasted concrete block wall. The Eames bent plywood chair, Guy Dill monoprint on the hearth, and 1987 painting by Ed Moses create an interesting composition. Photography by Erhard Pfeiffer.

RIGHT: Looking north from the living room, the concrete floor beneath the structural Douglas fir ceiling and beams, which have been stained, provides a grand send-off to the Alleppo Pine in the garden beyond. The doors disappear. The sound of water from a spillway at the Jacuzzi fuses indoor and outdoor spaces. Photography by Julius Shulman with Juergen Nogai

TWO COLLECTORS

TOP: Alex and Jaylene Moseley were eager for the house to blend in with the hillside, so designer Bob Moore used a grayed earth taupe color to let the structure retreat visually, as if in shadow. Along the top is a variation of the same color but lighter and with less taupe, creating a line of demarcation important to the architect in order to tie into windows and the line of his design.
PHOTOGRAPHY BY ALEX MOSELEY

RIGHT: Bob Moore selected the aggressively patterned 3 Rivers flagstone to contrast with the simplicity and serenity of the overall design. The irregular shapes of the flagstone make them feel as if found on site. The blocks of small gauged natural pebbles applied in epoxy are used within and without the pool for a welcoming dark but warm gray tone. Landscape architect Rick Fisher selected tall purple flax and Southern California native plants to fulfill the owners' goal of mostly zeroscape water conservation.
PHOTOGRAPHY BY ALEX MOSELEY

ALEX AND JAYLENE MOSELEY ARE BOTH CREATIVE, BUT IN VERY different ways. His interests are in art and design, including woodworking, graphic design, and video. She encourages and strengthens local communities through responsible real estate and neighborhood development. As managing director and board member, they work with Flintridge Foundation in Pasadena, which supports conservation, theater, visual arts, and community enrichment.

They both prefer spending more hours at home developing their individual pursuits than entertaining, and both share a strong interest in the visual arts, separately collecting tribal art from the Pacific Northwest Coast and Africa respectively. Thus when they asked the late **Donald C. Hensman**, **Buff**, **Smith & Hensman**, to design their home, highlighting their tribal art, including their 10-foot-tall Northwest Coast house post, was a prerequisite, as were a wood working shop, home office, and screening room. They wanted to take full advantage of their 1.6 acre site on a sloping hillside looking out over the Rose Bowl and across the San Gabriel Valley.

The openness of the main house on the relatively shallow, but very wide lot with unobstructed views, maximizes the spectacular view. Looking the other way one can see a protected pool court and a separate, more enclosed, and private wing of the house. This separation creates dramatically different environments from the main house.

Bob Moore, **Bob Moore Designs**, who worked with the owners on their previous house, was responsible for the interior design and all color. Landscape architect **Rick Fisher**, **Toyon Design**, helped the Moseleys fulfill their wish to use drought-resistant native plants and keep much of the original character of the hillside. The low-key appearance heightens the drama when one is within the home's expansive open spaces and surrounded by the Moseleys' highly personal collection.

PASADENA, CALIFORNIA

TOP: Commissioned for the Moseleys' previous Buff & Hensman home, the Northwest Coast house post carved in Haida style by Scott Jensen, Bellingham, Washington, depicts a traditional myth of how the rivers and lakes were filled with salmon. The architect designed the recess in front of the guest/office/film studio wing specifically to showcase the red cedar totem and accommodate its 10-foot-6-inch height. The water curtain is continuously recycled from the pool and provides a soothing sound throughout the open spaces.

PHOTOGRAPHY BY ALEX MOSELEY

RIGHT: The maple ceilings with alternating reveal hold Halo track lighting throughout the house for maximum flexibility and dramatic lighting of the art. Lighting is controlled by a Lutron Homeworks System that allows many programmed options. Concealed doors at the far side of the fireplace, at left, allow privacy in the master bedroom suite. The classic B&B Italia slate leather couch and chairs are from the Moseleys' previous home. Alex Moseley designed and made the coffee table of walnut, teak, and ebony with a glass base. The carpet is Boukara design. A Three Phase Chief Navajo blanket is used as a throw.

PHOTOGRAPHY BY THOMAS A. HEINZ

LEFT: The granite counter and range top have an oval bullnose, much deeper than the more typical quarter round cut and giving the stone a pillowy soft look. The stone is honed to remove the shine and make it dull like natural rock, yet it is still smooth for ease of maintenance. A scrubbable grayed-taupe matte finish laminate defines the wall behind the sink and has a ³/₄-inch glass ledge along its top. In the window is a Northwest Coast Haida style model totem by Scott Jensen. The deer antler was found on the property.

PHOTOGRAPHY BY THOMAS A. HEINZ

TOP: Interior designer Bob Moore selected strong purple and purple-blue hues in the living room to set up the Northwest Indian art, which is typically lighter in color. Also, the deep warm colors helped alleviate Jaylene Moseley's concern that the architecture's predominant amount of drywall would feel cold. Dark slate floors with Black Absolute splines counter the feel of the hillside location with a sense of grounding. Alex Moseley designed the dining table of walnut, cocobolo, purpleheart, teak, African padouk, and ebony. Dining chairs are by Stendig.

PHOTOGRAPHY BY ALEX MOSELEY

RIGHT: Examples from the Moseleys' collection: Northwest Coast Indian "Hamatsa" raven mask by Calvin Hunt, Kwakiuti Tribe; Northwest Coast Indian portrait mask by B. David, Tsimsian Tribe; and, in kitchen, Northwest Coast Indian Shaman by Francis Horne, Coast Salish Tribe.

PHOTOGRAPHY BY ALEX MOSELEY

ART AND DIPLOMACY

TOP: The library includes two chaises covered in soft handwoven chenille and contemporary chinoiserie occasional tables. The walls are covered with camel-colored leather tiles and the carpet is handmade wool of bronze background over-tufted with camel. Three panels of an antique black lacquer screen display rock formations and trees in gold.

RIGHT: The foyer is welcoming with a comfortable seating group upholstered in iridescent teal blue Thai silk atop a fine antique Oushak rug. The geometry of the black window mullions is reminiscent of the linear divisions of traditional Japanese shoji screens. The vertical blinds are computerized to adjust to the sun throughout the day. The self-supporting floating stair has a railing composed of solid sheets of glass capped by a wood rail.

THIS RESIDENCE IS THE HOME OF A HIGHLY SUCCESSFUL JAPANESE entrepreneur who operates on a global stage. He desired to build for his family a home that would act as an appropriate background for receiving the business people and diplomats with whom he deals on a regular basis, and that would reflect his broad-ranging interests and active lifestyle.

To this end, the client engaged Tokyo-based architect **Masami Kobayashi**, also a visiting professor at Harvard University who is known for his cutting-edge solutions to urban design problems. The new house was to be set into Tokyo's fashionable, but crowded Shoto district on a lot only 8,000 square feet. Kobayashi's solution was a dramatically urbane four-level statement with an elegant, but minimally detailed exterior clad entirely in flamed granite, and interior centered around a sunken courtyard that opens even the two subterranean levels to sunlight.

To soften the edges of this high-concept design in the interior, the architect worked with **Darrell Schmitt**, at the time a design principal with the Los Angeles office of **Wilson & Associates** before founding his own firm, **Darrell Schmitt Design Associates**. The designer was charged with the addition of straightforward but sophisticated cabinetry and material selections counterpointed with fine contemporary and reproduction pieces, as well as high-quality French and English antiques. The idea was for the house to feel as if sprung from Japanese roots, but with a layering of Western sensibility. Capping the client's charge was his wish for an assemblage of world-class art. Piece by piece, works were incorporated seamlessly into the overall composition, including ones by Marc Chagall, Robert Motherwell, Robert Indiana, David Hockney, Richard Serra, Renoir, Picasso, Kandinsky, Miro, and Calder.

Throughout the two-year construction phase, the architecture and design team worked back and forth across the Pacific. Along with the Japanese craftsmen who brought to the project their assiduous attention to detail, they indeed wrought a highly sophisticated and fitting stage upon which this cosmopolitan family can play out its internationally inspired lifestyle.

TOKYO, JAPAN

PHOTOGRAPHY BY TIM STREET-PORTER

OPPOSITE PAGE: The dining room walls, draperies, and screen are upholstered in highly textured silk in iridescent tones of gold and salmon. The expandable dining table and chairs are finished in highly buffed brown-black mahogany. The dining chairs are often slipcovered in monogrammed white linen, providing an extra note of elegance, as does the antique bronze doré and Baccarat crystal chandelier in the *a la Reine* style. Candelabra on the sideboard are also antique French bronze doré. The French bronze-trimmed parquet dessert stand displays various pieces of English Regency silver.

TOP RIGHT: The sitting room, reserved for the woman of the household, contains an office and an intimate sitting area for conversation and tea. Furniture upholstered in yellow silk rests on a contemporary French woven rug, and yellow grass cloth covers the walls.

RIGHT: The master bedroom has been designed with walls upholstered in pale ecru silk, matched in the tailored Roman shades. The over-scale kingsized bed faces a fireplace and hidden television across the room. The channel-tufted headboard is covered in ivory colored leather. Furnishings are a blend of styles from various cultures in contrasting finishes of silver, gilt, and wood tones. A Chagall lithograph hangs above a burled wood antique English chest of drawers flanked by Russian-inspired lacquer side chairs. In the dressing alcove, the built-in dressing table features a sterling silver repoussé mirror flanked by rock crystal lamps. The 1930s style chair with silver leaf frame is upholstered in un-dyed terrycloth.

AMERICAN WEST FANTASY

TOP: The view from the second floor game room gives a sense of how the living room and kitchen can work as one integral unit when a family and guests are cooking, dining, playing games, reading and relaxing—as happens in this activity-responsive home. Other features include: the living room's windows that can be folded away to open the room to the forest in fine weather; and a stone-clad fireplace which helps to warm the house in winter. A game table for two welcomes a game of checkers or chess. RIGHT: The heart of this family cabin is its dining room, with its lace-shaded doors opening out to the front of the home on glorious summer days and epitomizing mountain hospitality. The blackboard was purchased from a defunct schoolhouse in the Eastern United States and serves to welcome guests by name or define the day's menu. The chandelier is made of hand-bent copper and surplus glass shades from Italy. The room also has a wall-mounted dinner bell, so all can be informed when "Soup's on!"

SOMETIMES WHEN WE ARE TRYING TO EXPRESS OURSELVES IN OUR environment, we are not as clear about what we truly want as we think we are. It is as if we have not stood in front of our own "internal mirror." In this instance, it is much easier for an informed professional—rather than an involved family member—to help us separate our real needs and aspirations from our fleeting and often short-lived desires.

As a second home for a Phoenix family, **Eric and Dorothy Bron/ Bron Design Group** designed the Grosvenor family's cabin to evoke all that is best about the American West. The parents, Kathi and Steve Grosvenor, and their children Greg and Analise, wanted a space for old-fashioned house parties as well as a summer home where they could enjoy all that the outdoors offers in this woodsy, gated golf club community. They achieved this, plus so much more. In fact, when they asked the Brons to design a "little" cabin, the Brons, who designed the Grosvenors' city home and were aware of the family's legion of faraway friends whom they would want to stay overnight, convinced them that the "little" cabin should be a much larger retreat with five bedrooms.

In addition, the Grosvenors' desire for a welcoming mountain atmosphere was answered with spaces teeming with the traditional warmth of comfortable down-home hospitality. For the exterior, a handsome, but unassuming combination of wood shingles and stone has been complemented by colors that blend in with the surrounding forest and neighboring structures. Inside, natural tones are accented with warm deep reds, greens, and gold. Synthetic and exotic materials have been strictly avoided, whereas natural woods, leathers, and cottons are used in abundance.

The Grosvenors and the Brons found most of the artifacts in vintage shops and antique malls in the towns of Northern Arizona or Phoenix. Their goal was to have everything be typical of what one might have collected over time in a twentieth-century mountain home.

Although the house is far from small, all involved continued to refer to this mountain retreat with the same words the Grosvenors used when they first mentioned it to the Brons: the plaque out front reads "The Little Cabin."

FLAGSTAFF, ARIZONA

PHOTOGRAPHY BY BILL SPERRY

TOP: The entry area welcomes visitors with a hand-braided rug over the 24-inch x 24-inch copper-slate floor that extends throughout the first floor. A leather-topped table displays seasonal foliage selected by the owners. An antique saddle, riata, and rug adorn the beam at the front door. The pelt is among a vintage collection acquired by the designers for the homeowners.

RIGHT: Four rustic swivel barstools covered in red leather are gathered around the kitchen's antique juniper breakfast bar. The appliances are all up-to-date but have been customized to look antique. Countertops surrounding the sink are made of zinc. The forest-facing kitchen windows have lace shades for a degree of privacy and light control. The pot rack was custom made to the designers' specifications. The large island, which includes plentiful storage and a sink, is topped with honed granite.

OPPOSITE PAGE: In the bunk room bath, the triple trough sink and copper slate floor provide an inviting vanity for the many guests who visit this cabin. Storage, open and closed, was designed to be easy to use.

TOP: The living room's spirit is to do as you like: read, nap, and visit with friends on the generously-sized leather-trimmed chenille sofa. To the right is a complete entertainment cabinet for audio/visual needs.

TOP RIGHT: Double doors lead into the master bedroom with its bonneted-armoire-styled television cabinet and book shelves hand painted by William D'Sousa. The bed is made of peeled willow. An antique wagon hub has been made into a bedside lamp.

RIGHT: This bunk room is a favorite retreat on the home's second floor for guests staying for a comfortable night's rest. Fully occupied, this room could accommodate seven or more for sleepovers. Walls are humorously papered with "realistic" log-cabin-patterned wall covering. With recycled vintage wood floors, a window seat, and plenty of denim and flannel, the space feels especially cozy.

UPDATING TRADITION

TOP AND RIGHT: The rectangular living room, with French doors opening onto a terrace overlooking the garden, is so long that it consists of two separate seating areas. Wall-hung candle sconces flank the centerpieces of two opposing walls, including the limestone fire-surround designed by the architects. The Fango leather chaise and Wanda modular sofa are by Romeo Sozzi for Promenoria. Han television cabinet by Modenature. Leather topped coffee table: Hippo by Ochre. Kay floor lamp by Christophe Delcourt.

IT MIGHT SEEM UNUSUAL FOR A DEVELOPER OF MODERN RESIDENCES, but when he and wife found this very traditional semi-detached house, they knew it would be perfect—after first gutting it and starting from scratch.

The property was divided into bedsits—a typical British invention whereby the landlord would divide up an old house into as many rooms as he could squeeze in, throw in a sink, and rent them. The bathroom was usually shared. With this kind of house, the normal set-up is never changed due to planning restrictions and fire legislation. Thus, in this case, the layout was retained, with the kitchen/playroom in the basement, living on the raised ground floor, master bedroom on the first floor, and children's rooms on the top floor.

The couple is in their thirties, with two little girls. The main hope they expressed to **Chassay + Last Architects** and interior designers **Audrey Carden** and **Eleanora Cunietti**, **Carden Cunietti**, was that the house exude a sense of fun.

Some traditional features were preserved, such as the old wooden internal shutters and a huge attic space for storage. They kept the traditional old staircase as well, but also added a new one off the central hall and adjacent living/dining rooms that runs down to the basement. In keeping with such vestiges of the original structure, the new work was done using traditional methods, such as fumed oak floors and bare white plaster walls throughout.

Since the family was not bringing any furniture from their former residence, the interior designers were able to give everything a fresh beginning. This included bringing to the home a mixture of old and new with furniture and accessories from around the world, something for which Carden Cunietti has been known since the partnership was formed in 1996. Period pieces combined with stylish modern artifacts create an interesting juxtaposition: the quirky mixed with the beautiful, the strange with the rare. The main ingredient has been their sensitivity not only to the particular architecture—in this case the architects' neutral palette and spare adornment—but also using their sense of color, spontaneity, and great comfort.

LONDON, ENGLAND

PHOTOGRAPHY BY ROBERT GREGORY

LEFT: The kitchen is given a decidedly informal feeling with its oak table and woven hide chairs. Books and family photos on the built-in shelves next to the fireplace add to the desired sense of casual living.

TOP: Dark prune bamboo wallpaper by Helen Sheane sets off the dining room's Venini lilac chandelier. The three-ply sheer Roman blinds from Jack Lenor Larsen are in a fuschia tone, flanked by curtains of Zimmer and Rohde striped velvet. The custom bay curtain pole has a dark oak stain.

TOP AND LEFT: Bringing traditional warmth to the master bedroom is the gilt-framed mirror over the limestone fireplace, as well as the custom mirrored glass vanity unit with matching stool. Carden Cunietti also designed the bed, its fumed oak frame incorporating an upholstered headboard in cream-colored silk from J. Robert Scott. Other comforting textures include: the sheers of Sahco Hesslein Donata mohair, bounded by curtains of Jagtar silk with silver metallic trim; custom colored wool carpet with leather trim; and custom wardrobes in fumed stained oak with horsehair upholstery and leather panels.

OPPOSITE PAGE: For one daughter's bedroom, Carden Cunietti designed a playpod with integral toy storage, bookshelves, and a red-upholstered cubby hole for reading. The curtains have a cherry blossom motif and are trimmed with grosgrain ribbon.

NEGATIVE SPACES, POSITIVE FEELINGS

TOP: To the left of the fireplace, when sliding the *shoji* screen open, the garden is visible. The stepping stones are gathered from the property's 15-plus acres, and the single rock tied with black twine is a traditional way of announcing that a tea ceremony is in progress.

RIGHT: In the *tokonoma* is a discordant piece from China, because it reminded von Sobel of a carved Tibetan mandala. The other objects are the bronze two-piece traditional vase and an unusual short screen used in tea ceremonies. The rough cherry wood used for the *tokobashira* is grown in northern California. To its right is a small rice paper and twig window behind which a candle is always lit in homage to von Sobel's son Andre and late husband. Beneath a seasonal scroll is a box of Andre's writings, which Valerie has not yet read.

AS WE MOVE THROUGH OUR VARIOUS STAGES OF LIFE, OUR IDEA OF what design is appropriate to our needs often changes—sometimes dramatically. Or maybe we come to see that there is one more aspect of design that we wish to incorporate into our lives, such as a special place to be alone, to meditate. Surely those changes will echo our most self-nurturing thoughts and reinforce our attempts to turn even the most negative events into something positive.

Soon after interior designer **Valerie von Sobel** lost her 19-year-old son to an inoperable brain tumor, she established a charitable institute that bears his name, the Andre Sobel River of Life Foundation. Its mission that began in 1999 continues to the present, as does her passion for design.

Since her loss she finds solace in a design style that she did not practice in the past. Her current bedroom was conceived according to authentic Japanese principles. Having studied these values and ethics, she found they answered an instinctive longing for calmness that provides the healing for emptiness as no other.

It lacks color, but not texture; lacks noise, but not sound; lacks a multitude of objects, but not finesse. Seven different shades of white, the music of the koto, the raw fiber of the tatami, and the refined ceremonial vessels of the *chanoyu* (the tea ceremony) all provide total serenity.

This space is unlike her past designs, as it was born out of anguish. Instead of beautiful objects presented in eclectic splendor, this space shines by its omissions and by its use of negative space. The materials are foreign compared to the vocabulary of Western adornment, yet rich in other ways, such as the beauty of the bamboo, balsa, and paulownia woods and the intricate handmade *washi* and rice papers. The gnarled tree trunk that is traditionally grown for this purpose is called the *tokobashira*. It upholds the *tokonoma* that displays seasonal fresh flowers in the ikebana style.

Stepping outside and into the garden, you will find engraved on the largest stepping stone a fitting passage from the Talmud: "You are always alone. You are never alone."

MOUNTAIN CENTER, CALIFORNIA

PHOTOGRAPHY BY MARY E. NICHOLS

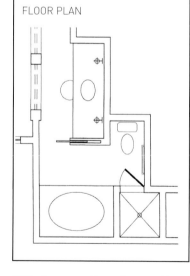

FLOOR PLAN

TOP: Opposite the small fireplace is a window to the bathroom that can be covered by unrolling the two exquisite scrolls. To the right of the *zaisu*, a Japanese legless chair, is a rain chain and two illuminated fiberglass sculptures. The stool, designed by Rund-Jan Kokke, is made of one piece of wrapped wood.

RIGHT AND FAR RIGHT: The various *tatami* covered steps elevate some areas above others. The bed, for example, is staged but, unlike for the purpose of drama, it is meant as a separation from the everyday by a step up. The woodwork is of soft balsa wood that is chosen for its light color. The bedding is of high count polished Egyptian cotton, and the billowing baldachin stretched between bars of weathered bamboo is of pale celadon. It is trimmed with the same fabric as the bed linen. The corners are distinguished by antique tassels, and the tip of the bamboo is lacquered crimson. The lampshades are crushed washi paper. The early

1900s flowers on the wall covered in pleated dupioni silk are made of shells and are from Sweden. They are a rare artifact made in the early 1900s by an eccentric member of royalty. Beyond the antique *shoji* screens is a low Japanese table with a foot-well underneath for

ease in sitting on the *zaisu*. Floor covering throughout is a combination of wool and hemp, except for the *tatami*, placed before the raised *tokonoma* area as well as the bed.

CONNECTING WITH THE ENVIRONMENT

TOP: The house is incorporated into the hillside to take advantage of the view toward the lake. The landscape design is composed of species native to the region—ash trees, holm oaks, and red grass—all enriched by the home's warm red exterior hue.

RIGHT: This interior/exterior corridor is characterized by up-lighted columns of carved stone from Valle de Bravo opposite a plaster wall bathed a warm red hue. The flooring is composed of Sangre de Pichón stone from the Red Quarry of San Luis Potosí.

TO **RICARDO LEGORRETA**, NATURE'S GIFT OF EARTH, WIND, AND sun—with color!—is everything. Thus, this banker and his family asking **Legorreta + Legorreta** to design their second home overlooking a lake, where they pictured enjoying water activities and their paddle tennis, was a natural.

Taking into account a terrain with a steep slope and a wide range of necessities, the resulting plan separates different volumes and places them on several levels as a connected piece of art. The divisions provide for the adults and children to have their own independent spaces. At the same time, the interconnection of all areas, always creating a flow between the exterior and the interior, was incorporated into the house as an important part of daily life for this exuberant, happy family and establishing throughout a connection with the lake.

The trees and vegetation are also important, complementing the architecture and providing all areas of the home with the mixture of sun, shadows, and color for which Legorreta + Legorreta is known. In this way, the house responds to its environment and offers a way of life in accordance with the climate and the culture of the owners.

From the front door to the garden and every place in between, natural materials have been selected to integrate the house with its surrounding landscape. The exterior façade is Valle de Bravo carved stone and exterior paths are red quarry Sangre de Pichon stone tile from San Luis Potosi. The interior is distinguished with marble, Salam wood, and lush hues of paint—the most predominant being the red selected by the clients from an array of reds presented by the architects. All is an overture to the glories of nature and the joy of life.

Architecture: LEGORRETA + LEGORRETA, Ricardo Legorreta, Victor Legorreta, Noe Castro. Executive architect: Alejandro Danel. Landscape: Eliseo Arrendondo.

VALLE DE BRAVO, MEXICO

PHOTOGRAPHY BY LOURDES LEGORRETA

LEFT AND TOP : The inspiration for the pitched ceiling comes from the old cabins of the region of Valle de Bravo, which were made completely of wood with similarly high roofs and wood beams. The accents of red, the window seat, and plenty of comfortable custom-designed upholstery turn the living room into an inviting, friendly, and cozy area for the entire family. Spacious windows and clerestories make the utmost use of natural light, while the windows' various shapes and sizes turn the view into a seemingly endless array of landscape paintings.

TOP AND RIGHT: Every bathroom has a glass dome and lattice windows. The skylights create the game of lights, an ode to Ricardo Legorreta's belief that light and spirituality go together.

RETREATING TO THE MOUNTAINS

TOP: Above a French country table is a superb French antique bunny. The Italian faience is also excellent. Chinese hand-painted porcelains are set against cotton gauze window covering and white hand-mudded walls.
RIGHT: The "Indigo Hour," so named by photographer Mary E. Nichols, lasts about five minutes, just enough time to inspire von Sobel's color selection for the living room's fireside chairs. Naturally fallen horns are made into a chandelier and hung on four chains in the style used in hunting lodges.

CHALET TOURNESOL, FRENCH FOR "TURNING TO THE SUN" FLOWER, is the idea interior designer **Valerie von Sobel** had in mind from the beginning for her inviting natural abode high in the San Jacinto mountains overlooking Palm Springs. She closed escrow on the property ten days before her husband died, and she felt intuitively that this was indeed the place where her husband would have wanted her to spend most of her time, as they both had planned to do.

She tore down the existing structure, leaving only the frame for 4,400 square feet of space for what she has turned into an extraordinary chalet. Every single detail is authentic, such as the kitchen window overlooking the living room, which she purchased from people living in a home in the south of France. It wasn't for sale, but when von Sobel wants something, she is determined, as people often are when enchanted by aesthetics.

Von Sobel believes a habitat should suit its surroundings, and that no elegance can exist without offering comfort first. Here in the mountains, at 6,000 feet above sea level —where, even in California, it does snow—a chalet-style high A-frame structure was most appropriate. A sky-lighted cupola forms the pinnacle of the soaring 23-foot-high central space that serves as a grand foyer/cum formal dining hall/library. The A-shape's gift of contrasting heights as well as von Sobel's continual juxtaposition of rustic and refined, makes shifting moods frequent in this home.

The color tones—including cognac, indigo blue, rich browns and golds and, snowy white—reflect the designer's intention that it should feel like a winter retreat at all times. So, too, does the abundance of chenille, warming embroideries, hand-textured walls, Aubusson tapestries, Ottoman objects, antique English silver, classic Windsor country chairs, and burlap! It is an embracing womb of sophistication and contrasts that makes you want to stay in its sheltering stillness where you feel warm and safe.

IDYLLWILD, CALIFORNIA

PHOTOGRAPHY BY MARY E. NICHOLS

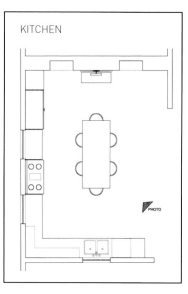

KITCHEN

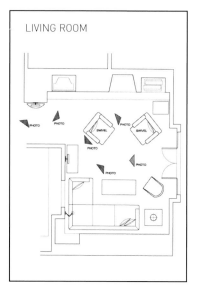

LIVING ROOM

LEFT: The sky-lighted cupola soars 23 feet over the chalet's entry hall, allowing it to serve as a formal dining hall. The height enunciates von Sobel's appreciation of dynamics of height, going from this extreme height to other areas that are mostly under 8 feet, emphasizing a sense of coziness and feeling for human proportions. The chandelier is a custom original, but the embroidered cloth on the round table is 150 years old from Spain. The petit point fabric on chair at right is English. The pale floor bricks are salvaged from a 200-year-old hospital in England when it was demolished. The house was built from antique wood from a New England barn, and that includes the floors that were milled and the rafters used. The pair of leather chairs from a Swedish men's club, early 1900s, are set against a backdrop of burlap curtains. RIGHT: A German still-life [1820] and window recovered from a home in Europe overlook the living room. The chair to the right is nineteenth-century Austrian. The Moroccan container below the step stool is made of quills and holds mail.

LEFT: In the kitchen, Windsor country chairs surround an old table from a monastery. Beeswax candles are used in the iron chandelier. This room is used for everyday dining.

TOP: Above the fireplace is carved: "Be still and know that I am God."

RIGHT: The gate-legged table is set with an antique English sterling tray. Above is a painting by Raoul Dufy titled "Carnival in Nice." The door to the left leads to the kitchen and is Indian.

FAR RIGHT: Iron grasshoppers on the balcony table—Valerie von Sobel's salute to life.

CONTEMPORARY PRIMITIVE

HOW DO YOU BUILD IN A PRIMITIVE MANNER WITHOUT IGNORING THE modern world? That was the challenge the young couple posed in the creation of a new home for themselves and their three children. More comfortable with the indigenous pastoral forms of their native Israel and the exuberant naivete of their Mexican and Latin American art than with polished formality, they challenged their design team to create a rustic structure unmistakably hewn by hand.

They envisioned a sort of primitive Mexican architecture with simple, strong forms, clear, sharp colors, and a strong emphasis on texture. They wanted something earthbound, but interpreted in a contemporary way.

Both husband and wife have a strong spiritual leaning. The house has areas of Zen-like calm. As they are both passionate, emotional people who enjoy entertaining their relatives and wide circle of friends, these aesthetically quiet areas are balanced with other spaces of outgoing energy and even tremendous luxury. They maintain home offices plus guest houses and a gym. The overall idea is to address functionally as well as artfully all the diverse aspects of their personalities in one multi-faceted but totally integrated whole.

The entire project team—architect **David Allen Smith**, interior architects/designers **Barbara Scavullo** and **Arnelle Kase** of **Barbara Scavullo Design**, lighting designer **Linda Ferry,** and landscape architect **Tito Patri**—worked collaboratively from start to finish. Throughout the process they involved many artisans—some local, others brought from Mexico and France—to handcraft every square inch.

The craftsman's hand is visible in the thick stucco and stone walls, the exposed heavy recycled timber beams, and the century-old roof tiles and limestone flooring from France. However, the owners were equally eager for contemporary counterpoints, an almost constant juxtaposition of mysteriously earthy serenity with surprisingly sleek modernity.

Traditional decorative light fixtures veil a keenly modern system of architectural lighting by which the passions of art, architecture, and interiors are truly revealed.

Despite the 11-acre estate's size (eight separate structures in addition to the 10,000-square-foot main house) it is, at its core, a home—a richly textured and powerfully expressive dwelling for this family and their passion for a specific way of life.

WOODSIDE, CALIFORNIA

PHOTOGRAPHY BY MATTHEW MILLMAN

LEFT: In the main entry hall, custom bronze sconces by Pam Morris Designs illuminate the dark ceiling while their placement leaves the larger wall spaces available for art. Punctuating the spatial simplicity is a knotted chair, Droog Design, MW Moss Ltd. The flooring is antique French limestone.

TOP: The living room's opulent, eclectic comfort contrasts with the entry hall's Zen-like simplicity and much quieter, more traditional feel of the adjacent library. The custom coffee table by Ron Mann, with its 3-inch-thick walnut slab on a Corten metal base, salutes the design's overriding theme of "primitive contemporary." Intense illumination is used wherever there are light-absorbing dark wood ceilings and saturated colors of art, interior furnishings and finishes.

Here, custom bronze chandeliers (their traditional cross-arm shape pared to its most simple form) brighten the potentially foreboding ceiling. The rug is an antique Persian Bakshaish. Late-18th-century Menerbe stone fireplace mantel.

OPPOSITE PAGE: Starting with the antique Spanish wood doors, the library is more traditional than other rooms in the house. With its saddle-leather upholstered niches, another deeply hued antique Persian rug, and floor-to-ceiling bookcases as well as the recycled heavy-timber 8-inch x 8-inch Douglas fir rafters and fill-in panels, this room could be darker than others in the house. The challenge was solved here specifically by chandelier, desk light, and downlights.

LEFT: In the family room, antique, all-cotton Kente cloths used on the sofa cushions were the designer's first purchases for the home. Their acquisition led to the assembly of a significant collection of vintage textiles, mostly tribal, from Africa, Afghanistan, Turkey, and Greece. The chandelier and sconce were designed by Paris-based Nathalie Hamot, who spent two weeks on site and worked with local artisan Jessica Bodner in their manufacture. This family room, an all-stone building, abuts the kitchen at one corner, serving the design intent of making this large property feel more like an estate built over a long period of time rather than newly built. The painting to right of fireplace is by Laguino.

TOP: Her retreat—a romantic, secluded space. The billowing bed curtains, inspired by colonial mosquito curtains, are emphasized by overhead lighting, as is the duvet, a nineteenth-century Kashmiri tent panel. Indian bone side chair. Venetian pendant. Antique Balinese mother-of-pearl doors.

TOP RIGHT: The powder room is simple elegance in a primitive vein. Font-like limestone pedestal sink custom designed by Barbara Scavullo Design. The blue, back-lit glass door of a recessed storage cabinet adds a whimsical surprise.

MIDDLE RIGHT: In the vestibule at the powder room, the scale, color, and intensity of the artwork continue to dominate, with spotlighting heightening the drama of a Tomayo painting over a singular bamboo vase.

RIGHT: In the master dressing room, there is a place for everything. A ladder accesses high storage for suitcases— always close at hand for this couple who travel constantly.

LEARNING FROM JAPAN

TOP: The new addition of the master bedroom fuses the new structure with the Japanese gardens and existing residence.

RIGHT: In the master bedroom, most items, save for the television, are kept enclosed within custom maple cabinetry in natural clear finish, detailed with mahogany. The floors are also mahogany, with purple heart wood detailing at thresholds and floor treatment at the base of the *shoji* screens. Purple heart is hard and durable, thus able to support the glides of the oversize screens.

WHEN THE HUSBAND AND WIFE WHO OWN THIS MIAMI HOME ASKED **Dennis Jenkins, Dennis Jenkins & Associates**, to create an addition for a new master bedroom, library, and bath to their existing home, they already had the aesthetic firmly in mind. They manufacture their firm's personal care equipment, household appliances, and tools in Asia, often travel there, and have developed a great respect for the serenity, calm, fine workmanship, and use of natural materials, which they have observed in traditional Japanese architecture. What they wanted to add to their meticulously maintained primary residence was a further design sensibility reflecting their admiration of traditional Japanese craftsmanship.

The purpose, in addition to having more space for their visiting children and grandchildren, was to integrate their residence more fully into the already Japanese-style gardens surrounding their home and the small lake beyond. The addition would allow them to take greater advantage of this beautiful location.

Due to Jenkins' research on Japanese architecture and interiors, he was able to blend it with his own manifest response to design appropriate to Florida, where he himself lives, with a spare but fulfilling interior space. Oversized *shoji* screens slide open along the wall of all the new spaces to lushly planted patios, lawns, and pool. Within the house, custom cabinetry and furniture of American cherry, maple, and mahogany woods, mostly illuminated by small aperture halogen lighting, invite every square inch to be touched and admired.

The resulting design lends itself to a pared-down look that evokes the idea of the traditional Japanese ideal, with most essentials kept behind cabinetry and only a highly edited number of significant treasures and defining colors in view. The striking combination of Asian culture, mixed with African sculptures gathered from visits there, and contemporary American paintings offers a blend of the simple, the striking, and the profound.

A quiet sense of serenity and calm flows throughout this home. The combination of cultures lends itself to the simplicity and beauty within.

MIAMI, FLORIDA

PHOTOGRAPHY BY LANNY PROVO

FLOOR PLAN

LEFT: The corridor to the master bathroom serves as a walkway through nature, its glass roof and window walls welcoming inside the sunlight and views of the garden. The paintings at left are by Dennis Jenkins.

TOP: Off the master bedroom, the built-in cabinetry of the dressing, vanity, and closet area contains every necessity, maintaining the sense of calm and continuity throughout the spaces established by the low-key design aesthetic and outstanding craftsmanship.

MIDDLE LEFT: Within the roofed portions of the pool enclosure, African artifacts stand as collected memorabilia from the owners' worldwide excursions. The wood deck covers the entire pool patio while the overhead trellis adds to the feeling of the handcrafted Japanese woodwork aesthetic throughout the house.

OPPOSITE PAGE: Black slate flooring and the maple lavatory cabinets with polished Absolute Black granite vanity surfaces create strong horizontal lines in the new master bathroom. The vanity and linen cabinets are constructed of maple with an open grain, satin finish with the tub enclosure of Black Granite. Accessories and orchids have been selected to embolden the Japanese-inspired aesthetic, as was the decision to minimize the distraction of cabinet hardware.

ODE TO SUNSHINE

TOP: The main villa features an oversized pivot door with Buddha handle and a clear view through to the pool. The lowered entry ceiling allows for the surprise of the soaring space within. Uplighting has been placed in the deck, but is augmented by candles for a feeling of lively hospitality and warmth.

RIGHT: The main villa interior looks up to a mezzanine lounge. The open staircase features floating Takien wood treads and stainless steel handrails. Upward lighting exposes the soaring lines of the roof. The space is, for the most part, left uncluttered, for a getaway feeling of serenity, to which a relaxing chair with foot stool and shawl is placed center stage.

FOR SOME PEOPLE, LIFE SEEMS PLENTIFUL BEYOND BELIEF, YET SUCH plentitude can become a burden if not carefully and thoughtfully directed in accordance with one's own physical, mental, and spiritual needs. A home can become a luxurious pad for everyone else, but not for one's own need for solitude. Or it could serve one's need for solitude, but not for sharing. Fortunately, through an enormous outpouring of insightful planning that elevates both friendship and privacy, this home serves both.

Located on a serenely beautiful beach, this retreat encompasses every aspect to enable one fortunate woman to do everything she likes to do on holiday: be it swim, sip cocktails, hang out with friends, or have massages. She had asked **William Lim, CL3 Architects Ltd.,** to design a party house that would incorporate a multitude of joyful aspects, with a main villa for everyone to congregate, but also plenty of private space.

A frequent visitor to Koh Samui, this Scottish-born Hong Kong banker loved the island so much that she purchased a coconut plantation on its west shore. Drawn to the Lipa Noi (Little Palm) Beach by its dramatic sunsets and spectacular views of Anthong Marine Park, she envisioned a home she had already named Ban Suriya (Sunshine House) taking full advantage of the panorama. Thus a U-shaped design was chosen so that every room would face the sea and the entire property positioned so that the sun would rise at the back, shine over the pool and deck area in the afternoon, and set over the sea in front.

The property comprises a main villa with elevated entry and four stand-alone private bedroom villas, each with its own bathroom and special water feature. The splayed-in plan allows each bedroom villa to have a view of the sea yet open up onto the central deck and pool area as well.

A different color scheme is used for each villa through the use of Thai silk wall panels and cushions. The Turquoise Room opens onto the pool—guests can dive in from the bed. The Lilac Room has a private deck capturing the best sunset view. Stepping stones in a lotus pond lead the way to the Fuchsia Room. The Silver Room has an outdoor sunken bath.

KOH SAMUI, THAILAND

PHOTOGRAPHY BY EDDIE SIU

FLOOR PLAN

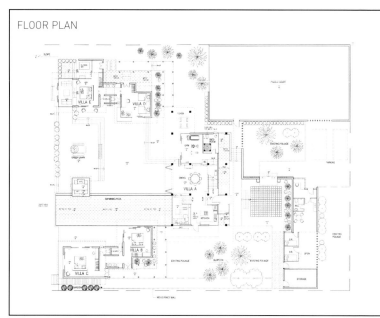

TOP LEFT: The double-height kitchen is fitted with stained plywood cabinets, limestone counters, and a stainless steel-topped central island with built-in ventilation. The tiered windows provide naturally controlled air quality.

TOP RIGHT: In the master villa, a raised platform separates the sleeping and lounging areas. Uplighting illuminates the lines of the pyramid ceiling at night. Teak louvers provide privacy. The few touches of color enliven, without disturbing, the overall plan for a restful retreat.

RIGHT: Along with a glazed ceiling to bring in sunlight, a structural glass underwater window wall allows the den to be below the pool level and allow readers that extra feeling of being ensconced in nature.

DIRECTORY OF DESIGNERS AND ARCHITECTS

Stanley Abercrombie, FAIA
Paul Vieyra
17273 7th Street East
Sonoma, California 95476
Tel: (707) 939-9117
Fax: (707) 939-9357
sonomastan@aol.com

Aleks Istanbullu Architects
Aleks Istanbullu, AIA
Arminda Diaz
Tom Nohr
1659 11th Street, Suite 200
Santa Monica, California 90404
Tel: (310) 450-8246
Fax: (310) 399-1888
aistanbullu@ai-architects.com
www.ai-architects.com

Angelo Luigi Tartaglia
Angelo Luigi Tartaglia
Via Boezio, 92 D/9A
Rome 00192
Italy
Tel: 39-06-687-3879
Fax: 39-06-686-8449
tartaglia.alt@tiseali.it
www.angeloluigitartaglia.it

Barbara Scavullo Design
Arnelle Kase
Barbara Scavullo
415 Jackson Street, Penthouse
San Francisco, California 94111
Tel: (415) 658-8774
Fax: (415) 658-5445
bscavullo@scavullodesign.com
www.scavullodesign.com

Bob Moore Designs
Bob Moore
2516 Greenvalley Road
Los Angeles, California 90046
Tel: (323) 656-8846
Fax: (323) 656-8843
bobmoore@bobmooredesigns.com
www.bobmooredesigns.com

The Bradbury Collection
Cecile Bradbury
8687 Melrose Avenue, G190-191
West Hollywood, California 90069
Tel: (310) 657-3940
Fax: (310) 657-5553
cecile@thebradburycollection.com
www.thebradburycollection.com

Bron Design Group
Dorothy Bron, CMG
Eric Bron, ASID
P.O. Box 32115
Phoenix, Arizona 85016
Tel: (602) 955-1053
Fax: (602) 957-4154
eric@brondesigngroup.com
www.brondesigngroup.com

Buff, Smith & Hensman
Donald C. Hensman, FAIA
(deceased)
Dennis G. Smith, AIA
1450 West Colorado Boulevard
Pasadena, California 91105
Tel: (626) 795-6464
Fax: (626) 795-0961
bsandh@adelphia.net
buffsmithandhensman.com

Carden Cunietti
Audrey Carden
Eleanora Cunietti
81-83 Westbourne Park Road
London W2 5QH
England
Tel: 44-20-7229-8559
Fax: 44-20-7229-8799
cc@carden-cunietti.com
www.carden-cunietti.com

Chassay-Last Architects
Berkeley Works
Berkeley Grove
London NW1 8XY
England
Tel: 44-20-7483 7700
Fax: 44-20-7483 7733
info@chassaylast.co.uk
www.chassaylast.co.uk

Cibic & Partners
Aldo Cibic
Via Verese 18
20121 Milano
Italy
Tel: 39-02-6571122
Fax: 39-02-290 601 41
info@cibicpartners.com
www.cibicpartners.com

CL3 Architects Ltd.
William Lim
7/F Hong Kong Arts Centre
2 Harbour Road
Wanchai, Hong Kong
Tel: (852) 2527-1931
Fax: (852) 2529-8392
william@cl3.com
www.cl3.com

David Allen Smith Architect
David Allen Smith
444 Pearl Street #D2
Monterey, California 93490
Tel: (831) 373-7337
Fax: (831) 373-1668
dasarchitect@earthlink.com

Dennis Jenkins & Associates
Dennis Jenkins
Sunny McLean
5813 Southwest 68th Street
South Miami, Florida 33143
Tel: (305) 665-6960
Fax: (305) 665-6971
dennis@dennisjenkins.net

Detroit Garden Works
Debra Silver
1794 Pontiac Drive
Sylvan Lake, Michigan 48320
Tel: (248) 335-8089
Fax: (248) 335-0860
info@detroitgardenworks.com
www.detroitgardenworks.com

Elliott + Associates Architects
Rand Elliott, FAIA
Brian Fitzsimmons, Associate AIA
35 Harrison Avenue
Oklahoma City, Oklahoma 73104
Tel: (405) 232-9554
Fax: (405) 232-9997
mjameson@e-a-a.com
www.e-a-a.com

GSC Design Associates
Andrew and Gayle Camden
552 Rivard Boulevard
Grosse Point, Michigan 48230
Tel: (313) 885-0767
Fax: (313) 885-5404
gsc-gscda@comcast.net

Hare + Klein Pty Ltd.
Meryl Hare, FDIA
138 Cathedral Street
Woolloomooloo
New South Wales 2011
Australia
Tel: 612-9368-1234
Fax: 612-9368-1020
meryl@hareklein.com.au
www.hareklein.com.au/

Julia Rezek Lighting Design
Julia Rezek, IALD
699 Mistletoe Road
Ashland, Oregon 97520
Tel: (541) 488-4254
Fax: (541) 488-9370
jrezek@mind.net

Kenneth Weikal Landscape Architecture
33203 Biddestone
Farmington Hills, Michigan 48334
Tel: (248) 477-3600
Fax: (248) 477-3658
kweikal@aol.com

Dr. Masami Kobayashi Archi-Media Architects & Associates
2-22-7 Daizawa Setagaya-ku
Tokyo 155-0032
Japan
Tel: 81 (3) 3418-7711
Fax: 81 (3) 3418-7800
mkob@gol.com

Landry Design Group, Inc.
Richard Landry, AIA
11333 Iowa Avenue
Los Angeles, California 90025
Tel: (310) 444-1404
Fax: (310) 444-1405
Richard@LandryDesign.net
www.LandryDesignGroup.com

Legorreta + Legorreta
Ricardo Legorreta
Victor Legorreta
Noe Castro
Gerardo Alonso
Adolfo Levy
Alejandro Danel
Palacio de Versalles No. 285-A
Col. Lomas de Reforma
Mexico D.F. 11020
Tel: (52 55) 52-51-96-98 ext. 133
Fax: (52 55) 55-96-61-62
legorret@lmasl.com.mx

Linda Ferry Lighting Design, Inc.
Linda Ferry, I.E.S.
P.O. Box 2690
Monterey, California 93942
Tel: (831) 622-7111
Fax: (831) 622-7411

Lisa Moseley Garden Design
Lisa Moseley
1352 2nd Street – Suite 19
Santa Monica, California 90403
Tel: (310) 586-1178
lmgarden@adelphia.net

Mae Brunken Design
Mae Brunken
6301 Quebec Drive
Los Angeles, California 90068
Tel: (323) 469-9069
Fax: (323) 469-9160
mbrunken@earthlink.net

McIntosh Poris Associates
Douglas McIntosh
Michael Poris, AIA
36801 Woodward, Suite 200
Birmingham, Michigan 48009
Tel: (248) 258-9346
Fax: (248) 258-0967
mp@mcintoshporis.com
www.mcintoshporis.com

Michael Helm Architects Ltd.
Michael Helm
P.O. Box 302900
St. Thomas, U.S.V.I. 00803
Tel: (284) 494-2135

Overland Partners Architects
Robert L. Shemwell, AIA
Steve Kline
Karin Shelton
5101 Broadway
San Antonio, Texas 78209
Tel: (210) 829-7003
Fax: (210) 829-0844
tbb@overlandpartners.com
www.overlandpartners.com

Paul Lewis Landscape Architecture
P.O. Box 260362
Encino, California 91426
Tel: (818) 788-9382
Fax: (818) 788-3217

Powell/Kleinschmidt
Thomas L. Boeman, AIA
Donna Edwards
Robert D. Kleinschmidt
Donald D. Powell
645 North Michigan Avenue,
Suite 810
Chicago, Illinois 60611
Tel: (312) 642-6450
Fax: (312) 642-5135
ddp@powellkleinschmidt.com
www.powellkleinschmidt.com

Richard Shapiro Antiques and Works of Art
Richard Shapiro
8905 Melrose Avenue
Los Angeles, California 90069
Tel: (310) 275-6700
Fax: (310) 275-6723
richard@rshapiroantiques.com
www.rshapiroantiques.com

Bruce Richey, Architect, AIA
1941 Westerlund Drive
Medford, Oregon 97504
Tel: (541) 773-4025

Rita St. Clair Associates, Inc.
Rita St. Clair, FASID
1009 North Charles Street
Baltimore, Maryland 21201
Tel: (410) 752-1313
Fax: (410) 752-1335
RitaStClair@aol.com
www.ritastclair.com

Darrell Schmitt, ASID
Darrell Schmitt Design Associates
6030 Wilshire Boulevard, #200
Los Angeles, California 90036-3617
Tel: (323) 951-9283
Fax: (323) 951-9231
darrell.schmitt@dsdassoc.com

Susan Brady Lighting
39 West 38th Street, 10th floor
New York, New York 10018
Tel: (212) 391-4230
Fax: (212) 391-4231
sbrady@sbldstudio.com
www.sbldstudio.com

Steven Ehrlich Architects
Steven Ehrlich, FAIA
10865 Washington Boulevard
Culver City, California 90232
Tel: (310) 838-9700
Fax: (310) 838-9737
cmonti@s-ehrlich.com
www.s-ehrlich.com

Tim Thomas & Associates
3239 Donald Douglas Loop S
Santa Monica, California 90405
Tel: (310) 313-6709
Fax: (310) 313-6711
tta2000@tta2000.com
www.tta2000.com

Tito Patri and Associates
Tito Patri
2801 A Union Street, 2nd Floor
San Francisco, California 94123
Tel: (415) 346-2226
Fax: (415) 346-2778
tpatri@earthlink.net

Toyon Design, Landscape Architecture
Richard W. Fisher, ASLA
206 East Meda Avenue
Glendora, California 91741
Office/fax: (626) 335-2534
ToyonD@Earthlink.net

Valerie von Sobel Interior Design
Valerie von Sobel
P.O. Box 15427
Beverly Hills, California 90209
Tel: (310) 276-1572
Fax: (310) 276-1962
vsobel@andreriveroflife.org

Whitaker & Phillips Decoration
Yoko Whitaker
225 Crossroads Boulevard, Suite 186
Carmel, California 93923
Tel: (831) 626-4559

Wilson & Associates
8383 Wilshire Boulevard, Suite 611
Beverly Hills, California 90211
Tel: (323) 651-3234
Fax: (323) 852-4758
www.wilsonassoc.com

DIRECTORY OF PHOTOGRAPHERS

Paul Bardagjy
Paul Bardagjy Photography
4111 Marathon Boulevard
Austin, Texas 78756
Tel: (512) 452-9636
Fax: (512) 451-9636
paul@bardagjyphoto.com
www.bardagjyphoto.com

Berger/Conser Photography
Robert Berger
2118 Wilshire Boulevard, #752
Santa Monica, California 90403
Tel: (310) 822-8258
Fax: (310) 822-2253
berconfoto@hotmail.com
www.bergerconser.com

Weldon Brewster
Los Angeles, California
Tel: (626) 296-0190
Fax: (626) 296-3360
Weldon@weldonbrewster.com
www.weldonbrewster.com

Santi Caleca
Via Cornelico, 3
20135 Milano
Italy
39 02-8738-2248
Email: santi.caleca@fastwebnet.it

Grey Crawford
Grey Crawford Inc.
101 North Grand Avenue, #21
Pasadena, California 91103
Tel: (626) 304-2646
Fax: (626) 304-2648

Cristina Fiorentini
Via Paracelso, 4
Milan 20129
Italy
Tel/Fax: 39-02-294-04770
Foto@cristinafiorentini.it

Art Gray
1717 Pier Avenue, Box 272
Santa Monica, California 90405
Tel: (310) 450-2806
Fax: (310) 392-7550

Mark Green
15 Highgate Street
Highgate
South Australia 5063
Tel/Fax: 08 8271 1134
markannette78@hotmail.com

Robert Gregory
1840 South Gaffey Street, Studio 536
San Pedro, California 90731
Tel: (213) 618-0927
Fax: (310) 547-5824

Jennifer Hare
34 Abernathy Street Seaforth
Sydney, New South Wales
Australia
Tel: 041-4-095-998
jenni@pioneers.com.au

Hedrich-Blessing
Christopher Barrett
Jon Miller
Robert Shimer
11 West Illinois Street
Chicago, Illinois 60610
Tel: (312) 321-1151
Fax: (312) 321-1165
www.hedrichblessing.com

Thomas A. Heinz, AIA
27157 Saint Mary's Road
Mettawa, Illinois 60048
Tel/Fax: (847) 281-9457
TAHARCH@earthlink.net
ThomasAHeinz.com

Aleks Istanbullu, AIA
Aleks Istanbullu Architects
1659 Eleventh Street, Suite 200
Santa Monica, California 90404
Tel: (310) 450-8246
Fax: (310) 399-1888
aistanbullu@ai-architects.com
www.ai-architects.com

Balthazar Korab
5051 Beach Road
Troy, Michigan 48099
Tel: (248) 641-8881
Fax: (248) 641-8889
studio@balthazarkorab.com
www.balthazarkorab.com

Eric Laignel Photography
530 Canal Street, #2E
New York, NY 10013
ericlaignel@hotmail.com

Lourdes Legorreta
Parque via Reforma 1920
Mexico D.F. 11000
Tel: (52 55) 55-20-96-59
Lourdes_01@hotmail.com

Matthew Millman Photography
Matthew Millman
261 Bradford Street
San Francisco, California 94110
Tel: (415) 577-3200
Fax: (415) 401-6902
matthew@matthewmillman.com
www.matthewmillman.com

Alex Moseley
1125 Linda Glen Drive
Pasadena, California 91105
Tel: (626) 585-0631
Fax: (626) 577-2704
amoseley1@earthlink.net

Doug Myers
Doug Myers Photography
600 Moulton Avenue, #306
Los Angeles, California 90031
Tel: (323) 227-6735
doug@dougmyersphoto.com

Mary E. Nichols
400 North McCadden Place
Los Angeles, California 90004
Tel: (323) 938-0662

Juergen Nogai
1239 11th Street
Santa Monica, California 90401
Tel: (310) 458-1250
foto.jnogai@gmx.net

Peter Paige
Peter Paige Photography
7 Sunset Lane
Upper Saddle River,
New Jersey 07458
Tel: (201) 236-8730
Fax: (201) 236-8732
peterpaige@earthlink.net
www.peterpaige.com

Erhard Pfeiffer
12405 Venice Boulevard, Suite 270
Los Angeles, California 90066
Tel: (310) 452-0096
Fax: (310) 452-9606
erhard_pfeiffer@yahoo.com

Lanny Provo
5286 SW 34 Way
Ft. Lauderdale, Florida 33312
Tel: (954) 964-6339
lprovo9@bellsouth.net

Russell MacMasters & Associates
Russell MacMasters
112 Cascade Drive
Fairfax, California 94930
Tel: (415) 459-8944
macmastersphoto@earthlink.net

Yona Schley
4, Menahem Itzhak Street
Ramat-Gan
Israel 52560
Tel: 972-505-540-780
yona@yona.co.il

Julius Shulman
7875 Woodrow Wilson Drive
Los Angeles, California 90046
Tel: (323) 654-0877

Bill Sperry
4239 East Edgemont Avenue
Phoenix, Arizona 85008
Tel: (602) 955-5626

Eddie Siu
Rm. 204-5, Thaniya Plaza
Bangkok, Thailand
Tel: (662) 231 2730
Fax: (662) 231 2732
cameracollec@hotmail.com

Sol Visual Development
Kim Budd
1395 Evergreen Lane
Ashland, Oregon 97520
Tel: (541) 944-9602
Fax: (541) 552-0347
Kim@solvisual.com
www.solvisual.com

Tim Street-Porter
2074 Watsonia Terrace
Los Angeles, California 90068
Tel: (323) 549-0121
Fax: (323) 549-0123
tim@timstreet-poter.com
www.timstreet-poter.com

Alexander Vertikoff
P.O. Box 2079
Tijeras, New Mexico 87059
Tel: (505) 281-7489
Fax: (505) 281-6631
avertikoff@msn.com

Nancy Robinson-Watson
P.O. Box 873
Castine, Maine 04421
Tel: (207) 326-4861
nancyw@manor-inn.com

INDEX